A Complete Guide to Horses

Monika and Hans D. Dossenbach
Beatrice Michel

BARNES
&NOBLE
BOOKS
NEW YORK

This edition first published in 1995 by
Barnes and Noble Inc. by arrangement with
Sunburst Books
Deacon House, 65 Old Church Street,
London SW3 5BS

ISBN 1 56619 952 2
M 10 9 8 7 6 5 4 3 2 1

Printed in China

CONTENTS

Anatomy and physiology of the horse 6

Introduction 19

Built for speed .20

History of the horse 22

The behaviour of horses 46

Breeds and breeding 68

Feeding 94

Stabling 104

Grooming 110

Tack 118

Health and ailments 176

Safety 188

Notes 196

Index 200

Acknowledgements 206

Picture Credits 207

Anatomy and Physiology of the Horse

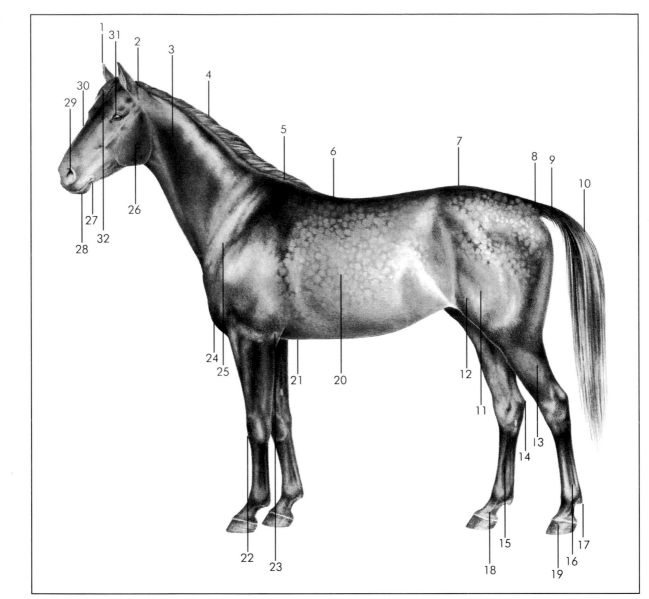

The Exterior

1 Ears	11 Thigh	22 Carpal joint
2 Poll	12 Stifle	23 Point of elbow
3 Neck	13 Gaskin	24 Chest
4 Crest and mane	14 Hock	25 Shoulder
5 Withers	15 Cannon	26 Lower jaw and cheek
6 Back	16 Fetlock	27 Chin groove
7 Croup	17 Ergot	28 Chin
8 Top of tail	18 Pastern and coronet	29 Nostrils
9 Dock	19 Hoof	30 Nasal bone
10 Tail	20 Flank	31 Eye
	21 Brisket	32 Forehead and forelock

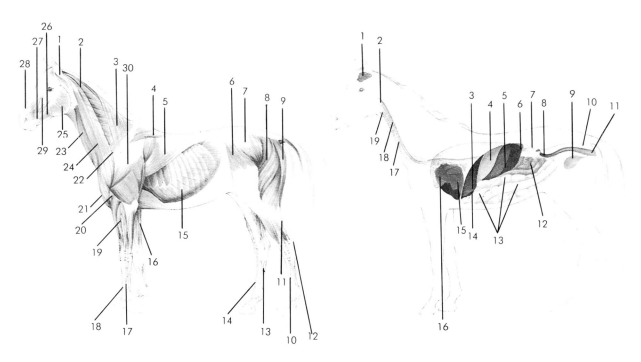

Musculature

1 Auricular muscle
2 Cervical rhomboideus muscle
3 Splenius muscle
4 Trapezius muscle
5 Dorsal muscle
6 Tensor fasciae latae muscle
7 Superficial gluteal muscle
8 Semifendinosus muscle
9 Biceps femoris muscle
10 Lateral digital extensor tendon
11 Achilles tendon
12 Superficial digital flexor muscle
13 Deep digital flexor tendon
14 Deep digital extensor tendon
15 External abdominal oblique muscle
16 Radial carpal flexor muscle
17 Lateral digital extensor tendon
18 Common digital extensor tendon
19 Common digital extensor muscle
20 Brachialis Anticus muscle
21 Cranial superficial pectoral muscle
22 Triceps muscle
23 Sternocephalic muscle
24 Brachiocephalicus muscle
25 Masseter muscle
26 Buccinator muscle
27 Orbicularis oris muscle
28 Upper lip levator muscle
29 Upper lip and nostril levator muscle
30 Deltoid muscle

Internal Organs (mare)

1 Brain
2 Pharynx
3 Liver
4 Stomach
5 Spleen
6 Left kidney
7 Colon
8 Uterus and ovaries
9 Bladder
10 Rectum
11 Anus
12 Small intestine
13 Large intestine
14 Sternum
15 Left atrium
16 Right atrium
17 Trachea
18 Esophagus
19 Larynx

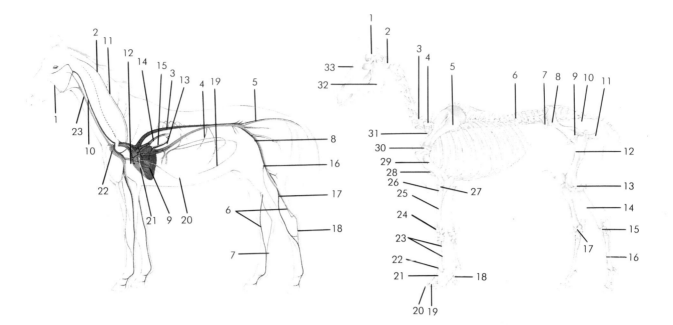

Circulatory System

The Arteries (red)

1 Facial artery
2 Vertebral artery
3 Aorta
4 Coeliac artery
5 Iliac artery (s)
6 Tibial artery
7 Plantar artery
8 Femoral artery
9 Left atrium
10 Carotid

The Veins (blue)

11 Cervical vein (s)
12 Vena cava
13 Pulmonary vein (s)
14 Pulmonary artery
15 Pulmonaric circulation
16 Femoral vein
17 Tibial artery
18 Medial dorsal metatarseal
    vein
19 Mesenteric vein
20 Splenic vein
21 Right atrium

22 Brachial vein
23 Jugular vein

The Skeleton

1 Cranium
2 First cervical vertebra
3 Seventh cervical vertebra
4 First thoracic vertebra
5 Scapula
6 First lumbar vertebra
7 Point of hip
8 Ilium
9 Hip joint
10 Coccygeal vertebra
11 Ischium
12 Femur
13 Stifle joint
14 Tibia
15 Hock
16 Cannon bone (metatarsal)
17 Tibial tarsal bone

18 Pastern joint
19 Navicular bone
20 Pedal bone
21 Pastern bone
22 Fetlock joint
23 Cannon bone (metacarpal)
24 Carpal joint
25 Radius
26 Ulna
27 Elbow joint
28 Sternum
29 Humerus
30 Shoulder joint
31 Rib
32 Mandible
33 Facial crest and upper jaw

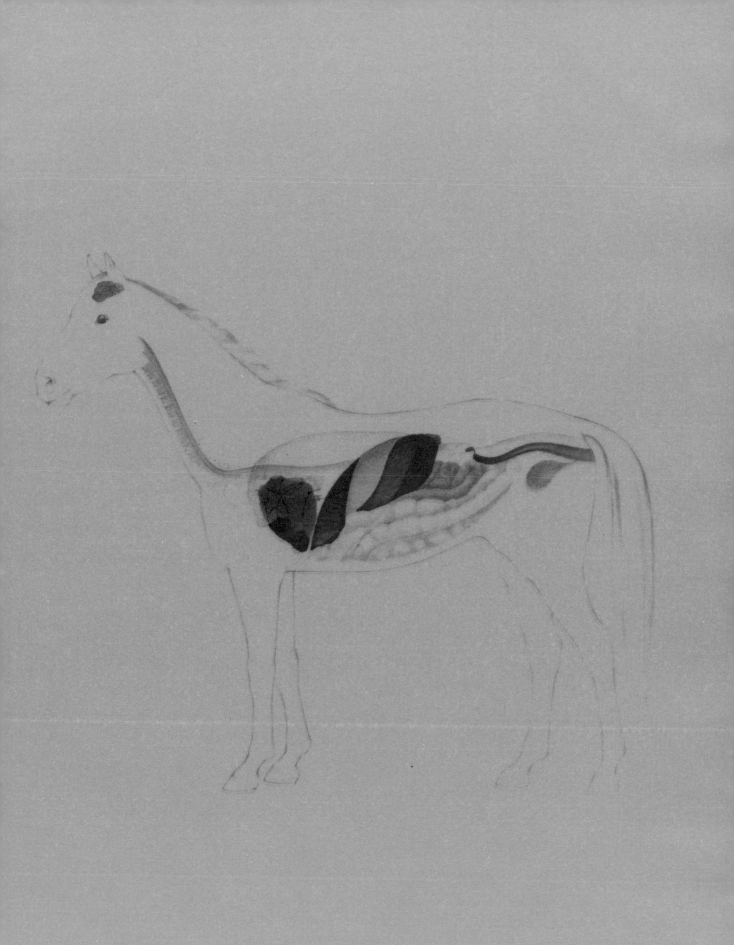

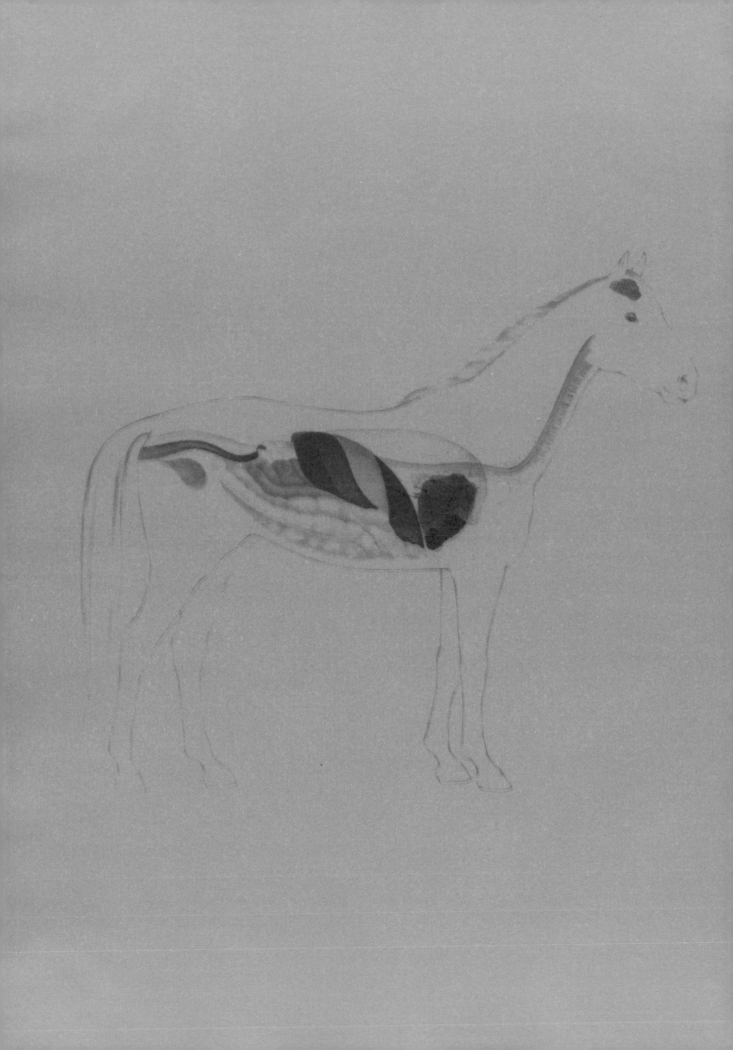

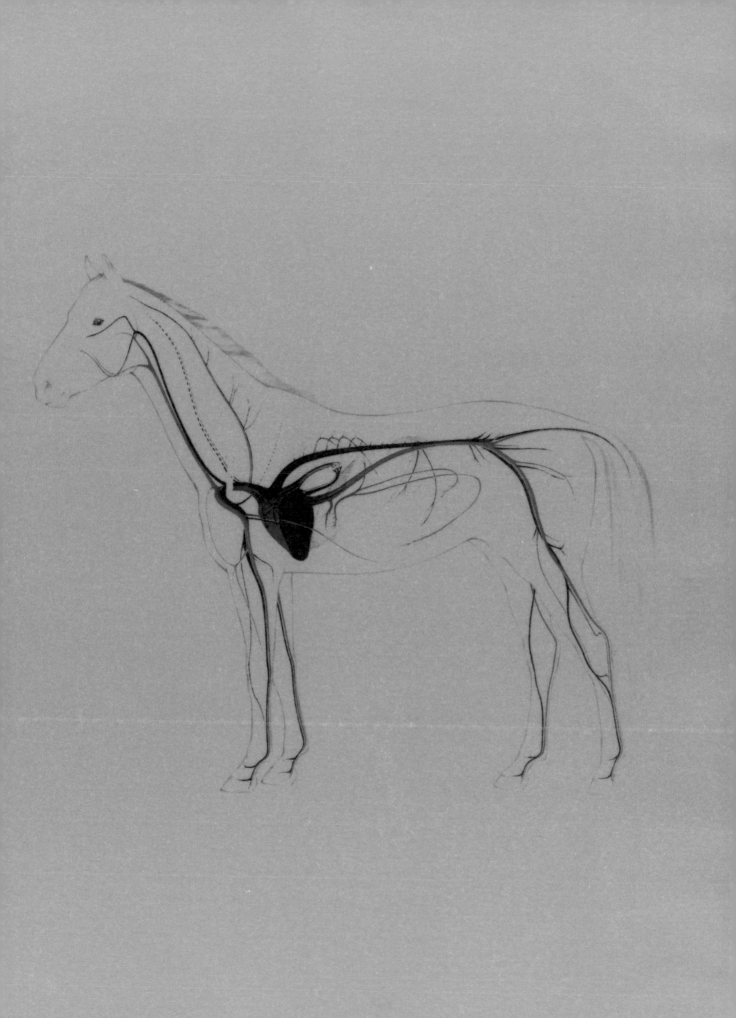

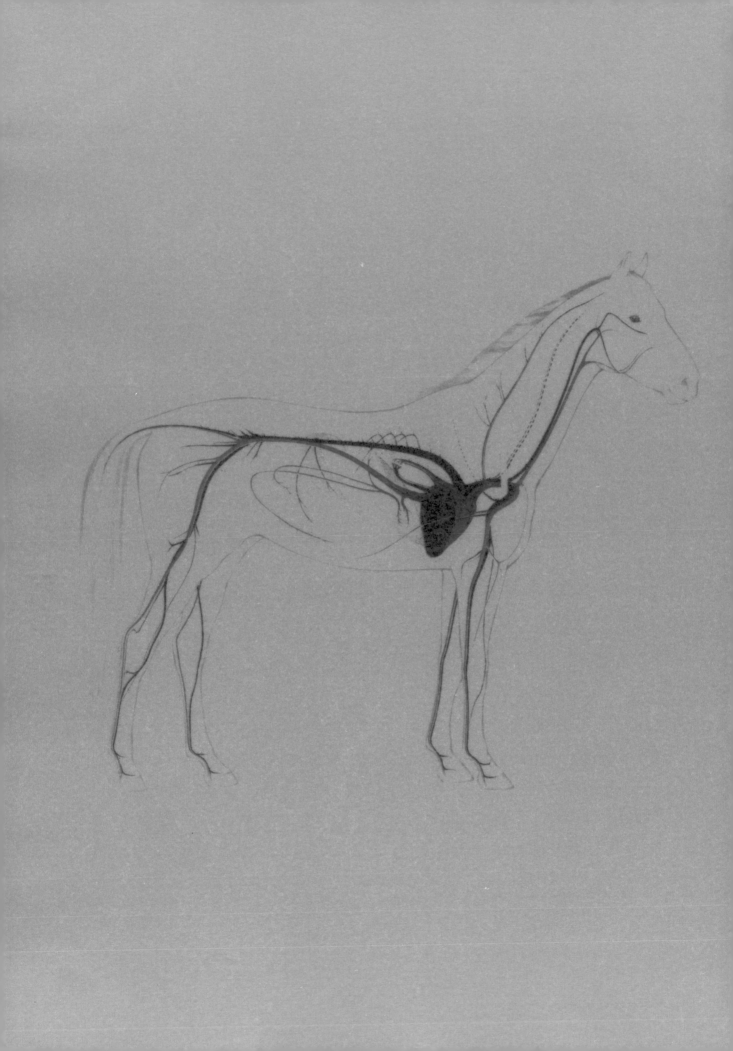

INTRODUCTION

Anyone, young or old, who takes an keen interest in horses will find this book a fascinating work on the subject, and one that provides answers to those questions which are most frequently asked by owners and other horse lovers. Throughout, the text is illustrated with beautiful and informative images, interspersed occasionally with amusing cartoons that nevertheless help to reinforce a serious point. The authors are experienced in every aspect of the care and maintenance of all types of horses, and by writing this book they have been able to share their knowledge with a wide audience in many countries. It is difficult to imagine a more comprehensive, authoritative and sympathetic work than the one the authors have prepared.

BUILT FOR FLIGHT

The horse is a fast animal; its whole body is geared to taking flight. A thoroughbred horse can run one hundred meters in under 18 seconds, and a good, all-round horse can spring from a standing position to a full gallop in a few hundred meters (a few hundred yards), to reach 60 km/37 miles per hour. Horses are also particularly superior to humans and many other animals when it comes to running over distances, particularly the Arab horses, which have the stamina to continue running for long periods without flagging.

Both speed and endurance have been essential for the development of the horse, for without these capabilities it would have become extinct long ago. Its legs are long and wiry, and the supporting surface of its foot consists only of a small hard hoof covering the single toe. The powerful running muscles that drive the horse are situated at the tops of the legs, close to its shoulders and rump. During the process of evolution, this feature enabled the lower half of the legs to become slim and elongated thus providing the horse with the ability to run at speed. Tough tendons, which are attached to the leg bones, transmit power generated by the running muscles to the legs.

Speed is of course significantly more important for horses in the open steppes and desert regions than for their relatives that inhabit that Nordic tundra and taiga forests, which are full of ample hiding places. Therefore the descendants of prehistoric horses from the cold regions, the northern ponies and heavy horses, are less geared to speed.

The legs of all horses are by nature also extremely sturdy, with the result that wild horses seldom injure their legs seriously

The Achal-Tekkiner, which originates from the central Asian steppes, is twice as fast as a sprinter and three times as fast as a marathon runner:

when travelling quickly across rough terrain. A leg injury would usually have catastrophic consequences for a horse taking flight; predators are quick to recognise when an animal is restricted in its ability to run, and will understandably take advantage of the situation. Domestic horses, however, quite frequently do have a problem with leg injuries. One reason for this is that, on average, domestic horses are about 35 cm/85 in taller than wild horses. Thus their legs are longer and are subjected to greater pressure, and consequently carry a heavier load. A second reason is that domestic horses carry people on their backs. On its own this would not be so bad if they did not also have to jump over obstacles. By far the most injuries to joints and tendons occur both in show jumping and in eventing.

Elongated legs necessitated an elongated neck, so that the grazing horse could pluck food from the ground. A long neck is also important for maintaining balance, and acts like a balancing pole.

The chest is particularly large because it must provide enough space for powerful lungs and a strong heart. In thoroughbreds the inner surface of the lungs through which oxygen is supplied to the blood is around 2500 sq metres/26,000 sq ft in size, whereas in humans it is no more than 90-150 sq metres/950-1580 sq ft. The heart of a normal horse weighs an average of 3 kg/6 ½ lb, whereas the heart of a thoroughbred can weigh up to 5 kg/11 lb.

Prehistoric horses of the Nordic moorlands, the steppes and the open plains, eat a rich diet of hard, raw fibres that demanded sharp incisors and, more importantly, effective and long molars capable of coping with heavy use. The horse's powerful chewing apparatus that evolved to cope with these foods determined the whole shape of the animal's skull.

When feeding, the horse selects stems and blades of grass with its flexible muzzle. Stems and leaves are snipped off by the sharp incisors situated at the front of the skull. At each side of the skull molars with sharp, pointed enamel surfaces grind against each other to crush the plant fibres, as the lower jaw moves from side to side against the upper jaw.

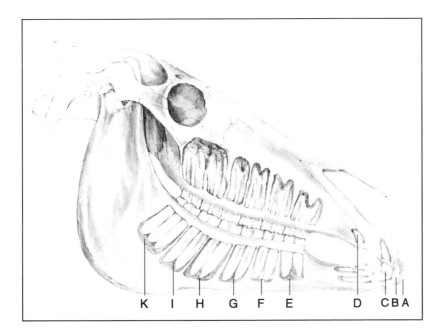

By far the largest area in a horse's head is taken up by the massive chewing appaatus with its long teeth. A to C are the incisors, D the upper canine and E to K the molars.

K I H G F E D C B A

Much more is known about the development of the horse than is known about the development of humans from the ape-like creatures that are our human ancestors. Palaeontologists and their assistants have dug up, measured, organised and described an untold number of bones of extinct horse-like animals. Skeletal remains, often found lying next to each other, provide clues to the ancestry of the horse, and many of these date back almost 50 million years to the Eocene period of Earth's history. This was the dawn of history, when a small rabbit-sized animal called by modern scientists *Hyracotherium*, (or, sometimes, *Eohippus*) began its evolutionary struggle through life.

These little 'dawn horses' would have been unrecognisable to us as the original ancestor of modern horses; it certainly had nothing of the fiery nature of an Arabian horse or the stature of a work horse. *Hyracotherium* had a hunched back and only stood about 20 cm/8 in high at the shoulder. Its short legs ended in feet with several splayed toes; and its small and knobbly teeth were set into a skull similar in size to that of a rabbit. This tells us that *Hyracotherium* probably lived on leaves and fruit, supplementing its diet with insects, worms and other small animals.

Hyracotherium apparently led a secretive existence among the vegetation of the primeval swamplands. It was an inconspicuous creature, giving no indication that it would some day have a significant influence on world history. Yet the little animal had several traits that would be of importance in its future development: an enormous urge to expand its horizons and an ability to adapt to changes that were taking place in the environment.

Hyracotherium's original home was North America, but from time to time it undertook massive migrations. Different forms of the early horse migrated to South America. Others moved across the Bering Straits via a strip of land that, until about 10,000 years ago, connected Alaska to Siberia. This enabled horses to move over Asia, into Europe and even as far as Africa, where today the zebras are the last of their descendants.

The horse eventually died out in both North and South America, the reason for this remaining a mystery. However various

Left: This prehistoric horse lived around 50 million years ago; it was discovered near the town of Messel in Germany.
Top right: 'Wild' horses of the African Namib desert, living as they did some 10,000 years ago.
Overleaf: A reconstruction of a small prehistoric horse at the Natural History Museum in Bassel, Switzerland.

forms of the horse survived in Eurasia, and these animals are the ancestors of our domestic horse.

But how was it possible for a small bush animal the size of a rabbit to develop into a large, swift prairie animal? During the course of millions of years the Earth's climate underwent frequent changes. The fertile, prehistoric swampland in which *Hyracotherium* lived dried out. Large areas of grassland appeared and then came the steppes and the open plains. Horses had the ability to adapt to these new conditions over a period of millions of years.

Splayed toes that had evolved to protect the horse from sinking into the swamps were no longer needed. The toes shrivelled to a middle toe with a hard toenail – the hoof – to enclose the foot bones and protect the feet. This small supporting surface enabled the horse to run faster. Thus the horse's whole body as well as its behaviour underwent different changes in the course of many generations.

Early human relationship with the horse

The relationship between humans and horses can be traced back to 20,000 BC, to the last Ice Age, and to the small wine-growing village of Solutre in southern Burgundy. Here, in 1866, archaeologists undertook a systematic excavation, and unearthed at the foot of a plateau the skeletal remains of more than 100,000 wild horses. Bones of mammoths, early cattle, bison and reindeer were also discovered, providing proof that the humans inhabiting the area at this time had been skilful hunters whose hunting methods included driving animals over a cliff to their death.

It appears that these Ice Age people appreciated the shelter afforded at the foot of this cliff, as evidenced by campfire sites, tools and small pieces of art which were dug up along with the animal remains. The horse bones which were discovered indicate that two different kinds of horses lived at that time and were hunted by early peoples: a small, graceful prehistoric pony, of 125-130 cm/49-52 in height, and a rather heavy-boned, 138-145 cm/54-57 in high tundra pony, which frequently migrated south to warmer climes at the first signs of approaching winter.

During the Ice Age horses were forced to avoid the expansive glaciers when they were searching for rich grazing land. Most

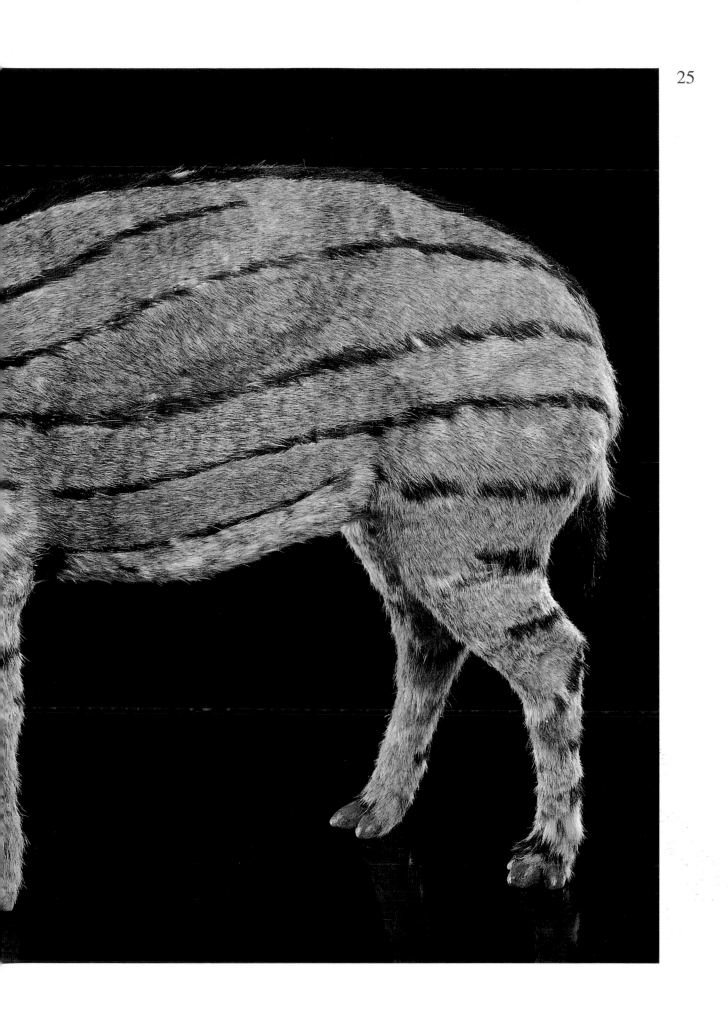

26 of those which found themselves surrounded by the ice masses perished; only those which could adapt to the changing conditions or move south during the winter were able to survive. A woolly and dense coat, an erect mane with no forelock and a thin tail protected the northern tundra pony during the long and cold but dry winters. This massive horse, which during certain climatic periods reached a height of 170 cm /70 in at the withers, was sure-footed; it looked for its food on the boulders at the edge of the glaciers and in the swampy marshes. In contrast the prehistoric pony in the south had a more delicate build. It had a high, raised head, a slender neck, a short rump and pronounced sloping hindquarters. In the damp climate of the Mediterranean its dense coat, thick mane and broad fanned tail were effective in repelling rainwater. The colour of its coat was a peat brown,

and it had a white mouth and a light coloured stomach.

But how can scientists tell, on the basis of excavations, whether the prehistoric horse had an erect mane or a flat mane or whether its coat was of a certain colour? The answer is, that for thousands of years they did not know. Then during the middle of the last quarter of the 19th century caves in France and Spain were re-discovered, the walls of which were completely covered with drawings of animals. The first Ice Age cave paintings were found in 1879 in Altramira, Spain. Here there are pictures of horses as well as other animals, including bison, mammoths and bears – drawings and paintings that are among the earliest-known evidence of human creativity. In caves deep inside the mountains, fully protected against the effects of the elements, they were able to survive for thousands of years.

Przewalski's horses: the quarry of Ice Age hunters were closely related to this species.

28   The European cave paintings allow us to understand something of the culture of Ice Age peoples. The oldest drawings are purely outlines lacking any detail. The later paintings, with their use of both strong and subtle lines, show the detail of manes, coats and muscles. Sometimes parts of the animals are painted in red ochre and charcoal.

Some of the most attractive and significant works of art originated during the last epoch, 15,000-10,000 years BC, at Lascaux, in France. In these paintings there are more animal groups in motion, and whole scenes of animals appearing in place of the individual ones. The simple line treatment with very little use of coloured surfaces makes the drawings highly expressive and demonstrates what an observant eye the artists had.

The finds of this time not only include drawings but also small sculptures and even entire reliefs carved into the cliffs. What could have influenced these artists and sculptors in their choice of this kind of subject matter? Perhaps it was an expression of the belief that images could influence the course of objective events. Tips of arrows are drawn on the bodies of many of the animals pictured; sometimes they are lying collapsed in a pool of blood on the ground – a deliberate effort on the part of the artist-hunters to catch the much sought-after wild animals through the symbolic act of representing the animal's spirit. The caves with the paintings served purely and solely as centres of religious cults or magic rituals, because they were never inhabited and were not in the proximity of any human dwellings. Some of these caves are located in places which are not easily accessible and visitors are required to do some dangerous climbing through narrow passageways in order to reach them.

The Domestication of the Horse

Further evidence of Ice Age peoples' relationship with the horse reveals that the practice of hunting horses for food was widespread, and that it was this that probably led eventually to the domestication of the horse. For example, a particularly revealing pile of refuse was found on the edge of the Dnjepr River in what is today known as the Ukraine. Along with the remains of camp fires a large number of bones belonging to cattle, sheep, goats and

These cave paintings are 15,000 to 20,000 years old. **Opposite:** A representation of a horse from Lascaux. **Right:** A horse from Niaux in France. **Far right:** The head of a horse from a cave in Asturias, Spain.

pigs were discovered, but by far the largest number of bones were those of horses. Here there were twice the number of bones than there were on similar sites of earlier cultures in this region. The hunters and farmers who lived at that time appear to have realised that it was easier to breed horses than to hunt them. A horse skull lying with the bones of a left foreleg in a ritual arrangement next to two skeletons of dogs proved to be a sensational find. Traces of wear and tear on the front molars of the horse's skull, which could not have been caused by natural wear of the chewing surface, confirmed that this horse had been bridled and then buried by its owner after it died. And next to this site the researchers later found two pierced pieces of antlers which had served as the side bits of a snaffle. Because these early people were not yet acquainted with the wheel, the owner of this horse must have been among the first of them to have domesticated the horse and to have discovered the art of riding.

The origin of the domestic horse

It was once claimed that all breeds of the domestic horse originated from the species called Przewalski's horse, but we now know that several different forms of wild

horse were domesticated. Some of these forms were very different from one another, in outward appearance at least. There were plump ponies, massive tundra horses, gazelle-like delicate and fast little horses from the desert areas as well as different types in between. All of these forms are what are called 'geographic' races (a term that evolved because they lived in different parts of the world), or subspecies. Yet despite the great differences in the conformation of their bodies, each of these animals belongs in fact to the same species.

The prehistoric species of the wild horse – and its various subspecies – has been given the scientific name *Equus przewalskii*, and it is this Latin name which is perhaps responsible for the confusion about the origin of the domestic horse. All wild forms of horse, whether they are tarpans, prehistoric ponies, early draught horses or thoroughbreds, are called *Equus przewalskii*. The first word in a scientific name – in this case *Equus* – always refers to the genus; the second word refers to the species. If yet a third word is attached, it identifies the subspecies or race.

The precise term for Przewalski's horse is *Equus przewalskii*. The steppe tarpan, which is probably the first ancestor of the domestic horse and a very important one at

that, has the scientific name *Equus prze-walskii gmelini*. The forest tarpan, which also inhabited central Europe and was wiped out during the 18th century, is *Equus przewalskii silvaticus*; while the prehistoric wild pony which died out a few thousand years ago, is *Equus przewalskii grazilis*, and so forth.

As a rule two different species cannot mate successfully. Offspring can be produced if two species are closely related to one another – but their descendants are almost always barren – and they therefore they cannot reproduce themselves. This is why a horse (*Equus przewalskii*) can inter-breed with a donkey (*E. asinus*) and produce a mule or a hinny, but this animal will inevitably be barren.

It is worth noting here that a mule is the offspring of a male donkey and a mare horse. A hinny, which is usually smaller, is produced from a stallion horse and a female donkey. All species of horses can be crossed in this way – this also means zebras with donkeys or horses with zebras and so on and so forth.

Breeding domestic animals was perhaps the earliest biological experiment ever undertaken by humans. After they were caught, the animals would have been kept

in unfamiliar conditions, where their captors could observe the effects of captiv-ity. It may well be that captured horses reacted favourably to their new living conditions and adapted with considerable ease. After a number of generations their new capabilities and characteristics would have been inherent in their descendants from birth. Breeders no doubt promoted this development by pairing off animals which individually appeared to have favourable characteristics, and in this way started building up large stocks of superior animals. Through total segregation from the original wild breeds over a period of generations, and through selective breed-ing, domestic animals gradually became less and less like their original ancestors as time went by.

Early domesticated horses would have been forced to adapt to new and above all more restrictive conditions. As time passed they became smaller in build than the wild breeds, a factor much appreciated by the breeders because it also made the horses hardier and gave them a more agreeable temperament. Through careful breeding it was then possible to produce horses from this stock which were even better suited for particular uses. For example, during

Left: This picture on the wall of an Egyptian burial chamber was painted around 1400 BC.

Below: An Egyptian king, shown in bas-relief, on the front of the temple at Kar0nak.

Roman times generals demanded larger horses to symbolise their elevated role in society, and large, massive horses were required during the Middle Ages not only to carry their riders but also to pull arms and equipment, which became larger and heavier as time went by. With the intensification of farming came the growing need for strong draught horses, whereas the horses used for transporting people needed to be lighter and faster.

Because of domestication a large number of the horse's original features have changed. For example, the brain of the modern domestic horses is nine per cent lighter than it is in the only true wild horse that still exists, Przewalski's horse. Other changes are more obvious, such as the enormous difference in height, the increase in the rate of growth and the much earlier onset of sexual maturity. Continuous hair growth – which produces an unusually long mane – a reduced hardness of the hooves and the variety of dappling and speckling which occur are also effects of domestication.

In some parts of the world domestic animals partially reversed the process of domestication – they escaped from human care and returned to live in the wild. But

because of the skills they had lost during the long period of captivity, many of these animals were unable to survive in the wild or to assert themselves among their wilder relatives that were living in the area.

Those horses that have succeeded in returning to the wild survived mainly in those places where their wild ancestors could no longer be found. However, not even these horses were able to revert completely to the wild form; the changes in their hereditary makeup resulting from domestication had been too drastic and had occurred over too long a period. Yet, in respect of conformation, size and behaviour, horses that returned to a life in the wild have a definite similarity with the original wild forms, as witnessed by the hardy ponies of Europe such as the Shetland and Exmoor ponies. In addition, certain characteristics that appeared in the early breeds have survived in those animal populations living in a restricted region. As an example, there are wild horses living in North America that still have the typical ram head inherited from their Spanish ancestors.

When people began keeping domestic animals, their lifestyle changed socially as well as economically. Unfortunately there are no known written or pictorial records from this early period of domestication that provide any information on the origins and development of riding in the early cultures of central Asia. However, archaeological remains of settlements and ancient coins found *in situ* give an indication of how much the lives of the people of those times were changed because of the saddle horse. Travelling by horse, they could obviously move further and faster than they could by foot. Evidence of such early horse travel is provided by items of copper jewellery that originated from the settlements of a different cultural group located 1000 kilometres away from the graves where they were found. The jewellery dated from the same period as the buried horse found near the Dnjepr River.

Riding not only brought remote cultures and languages closer together: it also promoted trade and the settlement of regions that until then had been inaccessible. It also influenced the outcome of hostile conflicts which inevitably ended in favour of the warriors fighting on horseback. But it took a long time for the horse to reach the Middle East and affect the lives of the cultural groups living there.

It is not until about 4000 BC that the horse ventured from the Eurasian steppes and became a draught animal pulling the war wagons of the Indo-Europeans and Semites. Subsequently the horse became the most important instrument of power for the people of the Middle East. For example, around 1750 BC rulers of the Semitic dynasty Hyksos were able to conquer Syria, Palestine and Egypt, their successes being considerably aided by their horse-drawn chariots. From the new rulers the Egyptians learned how to work with the horse and wagon and later were

Right: Assyrian horse groomers shown in relief. As early as 3000 years ago, the Assyrians had clay tablets containing detailed instructions on the care and training of war horses.

Opposite: Greek riders, from the famous frieze on the Parthenon in Athens, which was built between 447 and 432BC.

successful in using this skill to throw the intruders out of their country. In the 16th century BC the horse was taken by the Achaeans to Crete, Rhodes and Cyprus and from there to the Greek mainland. The Greeks were probably the first people who developed a more overall interest in the horse and not only saw it as an instrument for gaining supremacy in battle.

The golden age of the horse

The horse was held in high esteem by the Greeks. Its elevated position in the life, religion and customs of the populace as well as in the political organisation, its role in festivities and games as well as its military importance are revealed in a wealth of myths, stories and pictorial depictions. Of all the domestic animals a Greek owned, the horse was the favourite and was looked after with care. Horses were not used in the field; instead mules pulled the work carts and cows the plough. The princely horses of the day, with impressive names such as Aithe and Podargos, were used to pull chariots in races held in the hippodrome.

From the 8th century onwards the art of riding gradually replaced the use of the

chariot and led to the introduction of the cavalry and the sport of horse racing. Riders were carried on the bare back of the horse or on a saddlecloth: the saddle was unknown. Chariot teams in races and in battle were almost always harnessed with stallions. Although it was a custom with other peoples, castration was not practised by the Greeks. Mares were kept only for breeding or for the cheese produced from their milk. The main emphasis of horse breeding was on noble thoroughbreds. A widespread crime at the time was the stealing of good stallions for the purpose of improving one's own breeds.

The ideal Greek horse would probably have some appeal today: it had high hooves, smooth flexors, strong chest and thigh muscles, a bony head with small ears, high withers, deep flanks and low, flat hips. The Greeks were also the first veterinarians. On the basis of dentition they were able to determine the age of a horse, they knew at which time of the year mares would most likely become pregnant and they even knew that horses do not have a gall bladder. Milk, blood and the ashes of horse hooves and bones were widespread remedies for a variety of human ailments. The horse was also accepted into the world of the gods. So in Greek mythology, Poseidon is the creator of the horse Scyphios, which is capable of making a spring bubble with a blow of its hoof. Scyphios' son Pegasus, the winged horse, carries the lightning and thunder of Zeus. Horses are used to pull the carts of Helios, the sun god, Selene, the moon goddess and Eos, the goddess of dawn.

A World Power on Horseback

The first settlements of the ancient native peoples of what is now Italy were established in about 1000 BC in the southwestern part of the Italian peninsula. In the beginning these people carried out an active cultural and trade exchange with Greeks and Etruscans who had settled there. Following an Etruscan custom, they encircled their settlement on the banks of the Tiber River with a city wall – and thus founded Rome.

In 550 BC Rome came under the rule of Tarquinius Superbus, possibly of Etruscan extraction, who was overthrown in 510. The Romans later conquered their neighbours, advanced further up into their peninsula and continued with the expansion of their empire. Soon after the birth of Christ all of Europe fell under Roman rule (including what is now England), so that the empire stretched from North Africa and the Middle East to what is now Iran.

Everywhere the Romans went they found people who were successfully producing their own breeds of horses. But not all of the horses the Romans came across appealed to them. For example, they criticised the Arabian horse from Libya for being too small, ugly and thin, but at least they acknowledged its speed and stamina. In their eyes the horses from Spain, which had been interbred with the Arabian horses, were really more suitable for military use and for chariot racing. 'Fast, powerful, beautiful, pleasant to ride and responsive to the snaffle', these were the attributes the Romans ascribed to the Persian horse. The Romans understood how to use all the qualities of these different breeds for the purpose of breeding their own horses. They always bred the best horses for a particular purpose, mainly for the cavalry but sometimes too for transport and racing. These riding animals really

Below: A protective iron mask for horses made by the Romans.

must have been outstanding because, for example, for strategic reasons it was forbidden to export cavalry horses from Rome without having permission from the Roman authorities.

The Romans differentiated between three types of horses for breeding: the noble ones, selected for racing; mares used for producing mules; and ordinary work horses. The superior mares would only be put together with a specially selected stallion once every two years in the spring, whereas ordinary breeding horses were kept in mixed groups the whole year round. During the mating season the noble stud horses were fed grain and only the best

Below: A Greek amphora, on which
is depicted a young girl giving a rider
wine prior to a race.

hay. Their mares, however, were forced to find their own feed in the fields, because it was common knowledge even then that fat mares have a difficult time becoming pregnant. The breeding of mules was actually an industry, and exporting them was very lucrative for the breeders. The horse herds of wealthy breeders were driven into the mountains in the summer in order to protect the lowland fields and thus to have sufficient feed for the winter. Above all, however, walking on dry, rocky ground was good for toughening up a horse's hooves – something which was extremely important in the days before horses were shod. For this same reason the stables were to have hard, clean plank floors, because, as the chronicler Varro (116-27 BC) reported, 'it is important to be able to hear the sound of hooves in the stable.' In bad weather the mares were brought into the stables which, in extremely cold temperatures, were heated with an open coal fire.

Whereas slaves carried out the normal stable duties, well-trained grooms were responsible for the day-to-day well-being and training of the horses. The Romans expected a good groom to be able to detect and treat conditions such as worms, colic, lameness, hair loss, coughing and insect bites. His responsibilities also included daily grooming of the horse, something that was regarded more as a form of massage. The Romans knew that careful grooming not only removes the dirt embedded in a horse's coat but also strengthens its back and leg muscles and generally has a positive influence on the horse's psyche.

The only instructions on breaking in and training horses in ancient times which have survived from this age come from the Greek Xenophon (*circa* 435-354 BC), who wrote the *Hipparchus* and the *Cynegeticus*, guides for cavalry commanders and hunting, respectively. The Romans were great admirers of Greek art and life, and adopted many things from Xenophon's manual. They also warned people about such dubious horse trading practices as

Left: A winged pair of horses from Rome, dating from the 4th century BC. The horses were originally part of the Ara della Rogia temple.

Opposite: A Roman painting illustrating the abduction of Prosperina by Pluton on a *quadriga*, a chariot drawn by four horses.

stuffing material into the holes of the teeth of old horses to make them look younger. Work horses were broken in when they were two years old, racehorses not until they were three. In the case of the latter, it was recommended that they not be used for racing until they were five years old and fully grown, with well-developed muscles. But the training of a horse actually began when it was still a foal; after weaning it was brought into the stable and forced to become used to a snaffle made of a single twisted rope. The Romans recommended that sounds be produced using chains, cart-wheels and weapons so that young horses would become familiar with the noise they would hear in battle.

According to what we can infer from Varro's writings, Western riding is not an invention of the American cowboys – even the Romans expected horses to respond to a gentle shift of weight on their back or to pressure from the reins. Only one hand could be used to rein a horse so that the other one would be free to hold a shield or a sword, and the Roman military saddle looked like a prototype of the Western saddle. The Romans also had a form of temporary hoof protection, made of rush or iron, in the case of injury.

Recent history

What is known about the horse during the first four or five centuries AD comes mainly from military reports. For example, Chinese cavalrymen riding on horseback were successful in driving back the Huns, who had invaded their realm, but the Huns on their small fast horses conquered all of central and eastern Europe, making the whole of Europe tremble under their leader Attila (circa 406-453) and producing a

38 large-scale migration of peoples. The Arabs, who succeeded in bringing all of North Africa under their rule, conquered Spain in the 8th century AD on their fast desert horses. Finally, during the Crusades, which took place at intervals from the 11th-13th centuries, West and East faced each other in the Holy Wars: noble Arabian thoroughbreds against heavy European horses and riding ponies. The heavy horses had the advantage– certainly not because they were better cavalry horses but because they were mounted by armour-clad horsemen. Wearing coats of chain mail, armour and heavy plates of iron the European knights made themselves and their horses invulnerable to the hails of arrows and the blows from swords. However the equipment they wore restricted the manoeuvrability of the horsemen and of their horses. A rider who lost his horse during battle was also lost – that is if he even survived the fall. The popular knightly sport, the tournament, was also anything but safe.

The horse and the art of riding move into the forefront again during the early part of the Renaissance (14th-16th centuries). Using the model of the Greek Xenophon, an Italian by the name of Frederico Grisone published *Gli Ordini di Cavalcave* in 1550, which is generally said to be the first modern riding manual. At about the same time, Cesare Fiaschi, Grison's teacher, established a riding school in Naples where the sons of rulers and kings from all of Europe were trained in horsemanship. Over the years, Grisone's teachings were expanded and refined, and culminated in the famous *Haute École*

Pictures of knights from the *Tournament Book* of Emperor Maximilian I. The artist Hans Burkmair produced the coloured drawings around the year 1500.

40 (High School) typified by Vienna's Spanish Riding School, founded in the late 16th century. In addition to artistic figures in the *manège* (an open or covered riding area with seats for spectators) the great 16th-century riding master Antoine de Pluvinal also taught a style of riding which was humane, and applied a different approach to each individual horse. De Pluvinal taught that 'We should never smother the natural grace of the horse.'

The great riding masters of the past would no doubt agree with the following: it is only by knowing about horses and their behaviour and understanding their needs that you will be able to develop a healthy respect for them. The following chapters will help you to achieve this.

Le Bonnite, a 'barbarian horse'.

Practising for the *ballotade*.

Riding sidewards through columns.

Knee and thigh positions.

Tight voltes around a column.

Body position.

The Wild Ass, the Donkey and the Mule

There are two species and one subspecies of wild ass: the Somalian wild ass and its subspecies the Nubian wild ass, and the onager. In ancient times the wild ass appeared, among other places, in Asia Minor, Mesopotamia, Syria and Persia.

Whether the domestic donkey originates solely from the Nubian wild ass, a subspecies of the Somalian wild ass, or also from breeding with the onager is still a matter of dispute.

The donkey was domesticated earlier than the horse, probably more than 6000 years ago. It is thought that the earliest people to keep donkeys were the inhabitants of the lower Nile valley. In any case measurements taken of donkey skeletons found in Egyptian tombs indicate that they would have looked similar to the domestic donkey of today.

Even in early times the donkey was considered 'the horse of the ordinary man'. The reason for this may be that, unlike horse breeders, with few exceptions donkey breeders have never had any strong breeding ambitions and have only been interested in willing work animals, regardless of their colour, their shape or their size.

The earliest known references to the domestic donkey in Greece occur in Greek literature of the sixth century BC. The donkey was first used here as a pack animal in farming and by troops in the army; later it was used mainly as the power source of the mill-stones in grain mills, to which it was harnessed. The donkey was not much used for riding; this honour was frequently given to the mule.

The mule is the product of cross-breeding a horse mare with a donkey stud. This hybrid animal was well known to the Greek world much earlier than the donkey, mainly as a draught and pack animal for carrying heavy loads. According to the writer Homer, the Mysers, a people from Anatolia, 'thought up the idea of inter-breeding the donkey with the horse.' The mules were considered so valuable that they were presented as a gift to Priam, the last king of Troy: 'Yoke the mules with their strong hooves and put them to work, the ones which the Mysers present to the old man as a noble gift.'

The mule was so important for transport during ancient times that it became the most valuable of the domestic animals; breeding it was a source of great wealth. It was praised for its strength, stamina and longevity. Later, Romans who had to carry out dull, menial work ('donkey work') and legionnaires who carried their own marching packs were popularly known as *muli*, or mules, a term that is also supposed to have had the meaning 'idiots'.

A Mythical Creature that Heals and Destroys

The unicorn is one of the oldest-known animal symbols. Adorned with mythological and fairy-tale like features it appears in the cultures of Asia and of the Western World. Even though it never existed in real life this animal has not lost its special attraction. Fairy tales and children's books are proof that its appeal has survived to the present. The story of the unicorn originated in India, and is related as follows.

The hermit Gazelle Horn was born the son of an ascetic and a gazelle (who was the daughter of the gods), and had a single horn in the middle of his forehead. Having never seen any humans face-to-face, he lived as a hermit in the forest. Like his father before him he held power over the rain. Because the king, King Lomapada, deceived a Brahmin (a wise man) all the other Brahmins fled from his court; as punishment to King Lomapada there was no rain. The Brahmins prophesied that the god king would not allow it to rain again until King Lomapada succeeded in bringing the hermit Gazelle Horn to the royal court. The king devised a plan to use a young woman to outwit Gazelle Horn. The young woman who was selected built a raft near the hermit's hut and decorated it with flowers and garlands.

She succeeded in bewitching Gazelle Horn with her singing and dancing. Although he was warned by his father, the son stepped onto the raft of the young girl and was abducted to the royal palace. As soon as he entered the women's chambers it began to rain. The young woman became Gazelle Horn's wife and later returned with him to his hermit existence.

This story was repeated by travellers who journeyed to China, Japan and as far west as Europe. In the Chinese version the unicorn appears as a graceful part stag-like and part horse-like animal with one horn on its forehead. It was a popular decorative motif on pots, plates, bottles and fabrics. Called Ch'ilin, the unicorn is one of the four holy monsters, along with the dragon, the phoenix and the tortoise. It incorporates the ideals of goodness, honesty, credibility and wisdom. The unicorn is able to walk on water and land and treads so carefully that it never crushes a blade of grass or a living being. It appears to humans to herald the birth of a wise man or a ruler.

About 200 years after the birth of Christ the Indian story was rewritten by a writer from Alexandria, who changed the tale into a nature story describing the trapping of a unicorn. The behaviour and power of animals which actually existed, as well as those which were mythical, were described in this and subsequent nature stories, which were translated into folk tales in many different languages and were used to teach about nature in general. In those days the unicorn was usually depicted as an incredibly wild, powerful and unsociable creature in the form of a horse, with a horn that had powers to heal as well as to destroy. There was the firm belief at that time that the unicorn actually existed.

Not even during the Middle Ages was there any doubt about this. For example, a certain Vartoman from Bologna who travelled to the Middle East in 1503 reported that two unicorns had been caught in Ethiopia and were displayed in a cage in Mecca.

The traits of ferocity and strength which have been attributed to the unicorn have also make it a popular heraldic symbol. It was used as one of the emblems for Scotland and, along with the lion, was adopted as an heraldic animal in the English coat- of- arms.

The deep respect for the unicorn in ancient China and Japan was also based on its horn, which was recognised for its healing properties. The same magical powers were attributed to the unicorn's horn as to that of the rhinoceros, which was and still is a coveted trophy of many hunters. Proof that this belief has endured can still be found in almost every large city in Germany, where chemists' shops often incorporate the word unicorn into their name. In fact, many cities have even used this animal in their emblems. The best known example is Siena in Italy. Siena is divided into different districts, each of which is named after a particular animal or natural feature. In addition to the parts of the city called she-wolf, giraffe, eagle, tortoise or tree, shell and wave, there is also one called the unicorn. Even today these symbols are still used on flags and saddles at the famous Palio, the horse race in which the different districts of the city compete against each other. Young men on unsaddled horses ride three times around the fountain at breakneck speed. Whether it still has its rider or not, the first horse to complete the course wins the race for its district, where lively celebrations take place afterwards.

The Centaur -
Half Man, Half Horse

The centaurs are creatures from Greek mythology, creatures that are half horse and half man, with a man's body where the horse's neck and head should be. The Greeks regarded centaurs as demons of nature that came from the impassable mountains and dense forests which — inhabited as they were by wild animals — instilled in the Greeks a sense of fear and terror. These feelings were also applied to the centaurs of the wooded mountains, although one of them, called Chiron, was worshipped as the god of healing. Doctors made offerings to Chiron, who was thought to be the son of Kronos, father of Zeus. The Greeks believed that Chiron was different from the other

centaurs not only because of his origins but also because of his righteousness, gentleness and piety.

Like Zeus, Chiron was also immortal and was considered to be the teacher and friend of many heroic figures. But when he was accidentally hit by a poison arrow set into flight by Hercules his wound did not heal, and Chiron transferred his immortality to Prometheus. But to avoid wasting away forever, he voluntarily made his way to down into Hades, the kingdom of the dead.

More recent myths portray Chiron as a centaur at the arches of heaven, where he can still be admired in the form of the astrological sign of Sagittarius.

The Amazons
and the Feminine Art of Riding

In Greek legend the Amazons were a tribe of female warriors who had established a nation of women in the northeastern part of Asia Minor. Numerous Greek military heroes led campaigns against them or even attempted to abduct them.

The Amazons usually appeared on horseback, and, as they are depicted in the many illustrations which still exist, rode bareback like men. Oddly enough the French adopted the term Amazon to refer to women who ride side-saddle.

During Victorian times in the mid 19th century women usually only rode astride. Well-known cavalry captains of the time, such as the riding teacher Fillis of the Imperial Russian Army, wrote articles and riding manuals on the correct way to ride side-saddle. In addition to providing good training in riding, such manuals also addressed the issue of how young ladies should behave and dress properly for the sport.

Although women sat facing forward in the saddle like men, with both hips and shoulders parallel to the horse's ears, they were taught that both legs must be on the left side. It was thought that riding astride would rob women of their feminine elegance. It was also thought that women's thighs would not have the strength to cope with the hard jerk of the knee which was needed, and if a lady attempted it after all, she usually took such a bad fall that she would never again repeat this practice.

The female's riding habit was supposed to be tight-fitting but also comfortable. In fact, long corsets caused backache, and poorly-fitting headgear was distracting and prevented a woman from paying enough attention to her horse. Young girls were to acquire the physical suppleness they needed for riding side-saddle through riding practice or, more importantly, through dancing. English riding instructors at that time advised strongly against women taking part in fox hunting; this sport was not considered at all appropriate for young gentlewomen.

THE BEHAVIOUR OF HORSES

Many people think of horses as solitary beings which live in a box and now and then graze alone in a small pasture. In riding schools beginners are taught from the outset that horses should be kept apart from one another in stable gangways, on the track and when riding out, because they are apt to bite or kick each other. Yet horses appear to have a definite interest in other horses: they neigh and become restless if they have to remain in their stalls while their stablemates are being ridden off. It takes a great effort to get them to take a different route from the other horses when out riding; and even on the riding track they have an unpleasant way of sticking too close to the horse in front of them. The explanation given then is that horses are gregarious animals. But what is the real truth? And why do they have a strong urge to get close to other horses although they do not seem to always get along together?

Researchers spent years closely observing horses before they were able to provide an expert response to these questions. They specifically looked at horses which live a free existence, following their own inclinations and uninfluenced by humans. Wherever they make their observations, whether in North America, Australia or Europe – anywhere horses are still living freely – the horses neither want to roam around on their own nor do they always form a large herd. Instead the researchers observed that there were always small groups of horses with the same make up: an adult stallion with one or two, but seldom more, mares which, together with their foals and some 1-2 year olds, form a family. Occasionally two stallions would team up and form a family unit together. There

were also groups which consisted only of stallions. Because the animals shared the same living space, contact between the different families or between the families and the animals in the stallion groups was inevitable. They met at the watering place on their way to the resting ground or in the area where the best grass grew.

The initial impression was that the horses were forming a herd, but on further

examination it was found that the animals from the different groups hardly mixed together or that the individual groups sooner or later went their separate ways again. The horses within a family also behaved differently towards their own members than towards other horses. Special rules seemed to apply to the way in which horses organised themselves into families and kept themselves separate from other similar groups.

Among the closely-related horse varieties the Przewalski's horses, domestic horses and steppe and mountain zebras live in these kinds of family and stallion groups. The others – the Asiatic and African wild ass, the hinny and our domestic donkey as well as the Grevy zebra – reveal a totally different social structure. With these varieties it is only the mother mares with their foals, sometimes with a yearling as well, which form stable small groups. The stallions do not spend the whole year with the same mares, but instead specifically seek them out only during the reproductive periods. During this time they occupy a territory where they wait for the mares in heat. They will only tolerate the presence

Horses are very gregarious animals which, in the wild, always live in small groups rather than in large herds, and for their well-being need the company of other horses. This is something which must be taken into consideration when keeping horses.

of other stallions in the same area if the latter show submission; serious competitors for the favours of females are chased away immediately. Alternatively, stallions escort the females which are in heat and protect them against any other stallions with the same intentions.

Outside the reproductive period it appears that both mares and stallions sometimes join together to form large mixed groups. In the case of the Grevy zebra, for example, these groups can increase to include several hundred animals, thus becoming real herds. The animals in these groups come and go as they like; they only stay with a group for a few hours or for several days and then go their own way or join up with other groups. No close relationships exist between the adult animals nor are there any strict rules applied for the time they spend together. It is assumed that this herd formation is encouraged by the plentiful and dependable food supplies regularly found during the rainy season in the large African steppes and savannahs. When food is more difficult to find during the dry season the animals adapt and only roam through the area in pairs or in small groups. Actually each one of these animals is always free to go its own way. But latching on to other animals for a certain period of time has its advantages: a group provides more protection against enemies. For example, members of a group can take turns keeping a watch on their surroundings and see in advance whether any predatory enemies are creeping up on them.

Horse relationships are totally different. After years of observation behavioural scientists established that the adult animals in a family normally stay together for as long as the horses live. The only time the situation changes is if one of the horses dies, a mare is abducted or a stallion in the family unit is replaced by another stallion. Because the reproductive period for horses is relatively long, from March to September, it is apparently more advantageous for a stallion to capture one or two mares and keep them; otherwise it would have to spend most of its time looking for a mare in heat and protecting it, successfully or not, from other stallions. This would take a great deal of effort, have risks attached to it and would take valuable time away from looking for food to eat. The number of mares in a family is remarkably constant; it varies between two and three. This number is not even exceeded in areas where good feeding is available, indicating that under normal circumstances a stallion is not in a position to capture more mares and to protect them from other stallions.

As a consequence of these stable relationships the stallion will almost always mate with the mares within its own family. But it does not only take on the father role for the foals born in its family; it also has a great influence on other matters. For example, the mares and young animals must obey when the stallion drives them in a particular direction; they also must move aside and make room for the stallion if it insists on sitting down with them. However, the stallion often allows its mares to make the decisions on where and how long to eat and rest.

A pecking order also exists among the mares within a horse family. Almost always at the head is the oldest mare which is allowed to have the best foraging places and to be the first to drink at the water hole. This supremacy is usually recognised by the others; otherwise a threatening gesture is enough to ensure that a lower-ranking mare will immediately give way. The young animals must always make way for the older ones and are only allowed to dominate the ones younger than themselves. The foals are right at the bottom of the hierarchy. This means that a foal should actually give precedence to all other horses, although in the presence of its mother it benefits from her position. It is allowed to rub its coat on the rolling ground immediately after her and will not be chased away by the waiting old mares; its mother will signal to the others that they are not to push forward until her young one has finished.

The role of the father and pecking order only contribute partly to the diverse relationships which exist between the family members. The horses within a family know each other very well and are familiar with each other's peculiarities, strengths and weaknesses. Each horse which belongs to the group shares the same living space and knows where its place is within the community. It also acts as a friend and partner to the others. The amount of time the family spends together strengthens the relationships within it. Day and night, and for years as adults, the horses live side-by-side with each other. They have such a strong and exclusive friendship that other horses have a difficult time being accepted into their circle. Whatever they are doing – whether they are feeding, resting, rolling on the ground or roaming – they never lose sight of each other. If they are separated, they will not settle down until they have found each other again. They follow each other everywhere and always want to be close to one other; they touch frequently and help each other to keep the insects away; they 'rub' each other's coats.

Above: A horse family usually consists of a stallion, two or three mares and a foal.
Overleaf: An eager young stallion searching for mares with which to establish a new family.

Above: Being in a group gives horses a sense of security. While some of the animals keep watch, the others can feel safe taking a rest.

The behaviour of horses living in the wild has important implications for the domesticated horse. If domesticated horses did not live by hierarchic rules, their owners would not stand a chance of asserting themselves against these physically far stronger animals. Already during the early stages of its development a young horse will learn to accept people as higher-ranking beings. For example, once established, relationships of rank rigidly apply: seldom do the positions change. Minor quarrels about rank rarely lead to major fights but instead are settled simply through the special mannerisms displayed by the higher-ranking horse. This is why horse owners do not have to show their horse repeatedly that the owner occupies a higher rank. A self-assured, determined and sometimes forceful manner is all it takes. If the horse lives in a community with other horses, its integration into the horse hierarchy should be made easier for it. This will make it feel more secure and let it know what kind of reaction to expect from other horses in the event of a conflict. Conflicts cannot be avoided in open stables where horses have freedom of movement. It is also advantageous for the horse to know the position held by each of the other horses. It is important to ensure that lower-ranking horses do not come off too badly in the company of the others. They are not in a position to make way for other horses during feeding or to seek food elsewhere. An understanding of their pecking order is also important when a horse is being groomed and saddled, as well as when it is being ridden on the track or exercised.

A horse's position within the horse community and the owner's role of superiority constitute only some of the relationships which can exist. In the life of a horse friendship also plays a very important part. Of course this can be of a more diverse nature in natural communities than in the usual situations in which horses are kept. Friendly relationships exist not only between a stallion and its mares but also among the mares themselves, between them and their offspring or among the stallions which live in their own groups. Horses change their partners during the course of their youth. Naturally when they are foals they have a close relationship with their mothers which with time then extends to their older siblings. As they grow older they develop more of an interest in horses of the same age, with young stallions and young mares preferring the company of their own sex. As adult animals they remain loyal to the partners they chose earlier. As different as the partners in the life of a horse can be, the significance of their friendships always remains the same. Therefore a horse of any age or gender is capable of friendship and also looks for it its whole life long. Horses in the care of humans are the fortunate ones because they are able to live together with other horses. They can even choose their own mates and, if they have understanding owners, continue these relationships for their entire life.

Horses are so tolerant that they even accept humans as friends and partners. However, it is not possible to become a

Right: Rolling is a natural need of horses. It is usually 'contagious' and excites other animals in the group to roll too.

54 friend to your horse overnight – and certainly never because you feed it. To build the right kind of friendship you need to spend time with your horse; your company in the stable or at its side in a field can be a replacement for the family with which your horse would normally be grazing or resting. Horses that like each other follow each other around everywhere; on long rides show your horse that you are looking for its friendship. Stay still and do not reject it when it wants to rub its head against you; what it is doing is showing its affection for you. Take your time when you are grooming your horse and, above all, give special attention to the areas around the withers and the back. These are the places a horse is not able to reach itself and where friends among a group of horses rub each other. If your horse has understood your intentions, you have to take care: because it is natural for a horse to clean its partners, it will try to clean you. When this happens, turn its head away, lovingly but firmly, and make it clear to your horse that this favour is not wanted. By the way, scratching the area at the side of the withers is also an excellent way to calm a restless or excited horse. When your horse reacts to your arrival one day with happy neighing or detaches itself from the other horses in the meadow to greet you, you will then know you have made a loyal friend. And do not take your friendship away from your horse without good reason. You should remain friends for a lifetime and on a reciprocal basis.

Communication

Horses have many different ways of communicating with other horses and with humans. Their facial expressions, the way they hold their head and neck and the whole posture of their body contribute towards the language that they use for

Right and below: Young horses change their relationships often. Friendships between adult horses, however, endure over many years and guarantee that a group stays together.

56 conveying friendship, superiority, rivalry, protectiveness, caring and many other things. For the most part they do not have to learn their body movements and gestures; even young foals are aware of what they mean. Anyone who has dealt with horses will surely have seen the look on a horse's face as it keenly and inquisitively inspects its surroundings. It stands still, throws back its head, widens its

nostrils so it can also experience the smell of its surroundings, has a fixed stare and pricks its ears. These are actually all part of the horse's mood barometer. Pricked ears pointed forwards indicate attentiveness and a willingness to make contact. When its ears hang down slightly to the side and its eyes are half closed it means that a horse is dozing. With its ears flattened down towards the back it is threatening or

Horses of the Camargue. The head horse determines when the group will break up and in which direction it will ride; it always leads the others. Despite the strict pecking order there is a friendly relationship between the horses.

58 expressing its displeasure at something. When it is in this mood, it narrows its nostrils, pulls back its mouth and tenses its facial muscles. This expression on its face is also a sign that the horse is about ready to kick out with its back hooves. Incidentally, mares tend to kick out with their hind legs more frequently than stallions which are more apt to deal with their quarrels frontally – rearing, biting and hitting with their fore legs. If a threatening look on its face does not produce the desired results, a horse will make its intentions even clearer: it opens its mouth and shows its incisors. Anyone who has not got the message and refuses to get out of its way runs the risk of being badly bitten.

Family stallions display a certain behaviour when they want to lead their mares in a certain direction. They not only produce a threatening look but also emphasise this expression by extending their neck and lowering their head almost to the ground, moving it back and forth towards the direction they want to go. One of the most conspicuous faces is the one of young horses showing 'an underdog chewing look'. Lowering their head and neck they open up their mouth, bare their incisors and chew away in a clearly exaggerated manner although they have nothing in their mouth. While doing this they sometimes also buckle their front legs to make themselves appear smaller and they also pull in their tails.

Young animals, above all young stallions, resort to this kind of mimicry when they are threatened by the family stallion, cross its path or greet it. It appears to be an appeasing gesture – in any case it seems to put a stop to stronger threatening gestures. A signal is given to the older horse that the younger one is not questioning its superior position. Foals which lose their way and end up with the wrong mares or shrink back from a difficult passage or ditch filled with water will also show this look on their faces. This probably conveys a feeling of general insecurity.

Horses do not use their ears only to indicate their mood; they can also hear extremely well – in fact, better than humans can. With their long necks and movable external ears they are easily able

Left: The 'language' of horses contains acoustic signals, such as neighing, which allows them to communicate with other horses over large distances.
Right: When horses detect a particularly interesting scent, they curl back their lips, which is called fleering. This is how they absorb the smells into a special olfactory organ (Jacobson's organ).

Above: A hearty yawn.

Below: A threatening gesture is usually enough, but sometimes it takes a fast bite to show who is the boss.

to locate sounds. And they can tell which horse is neighing, even if it is far away or out of sight. The further horses are away from each other, the louder they call out to one another. However, animals which know each other well and meet again after a long separation greet each another with short, deep sounds. A mother will also answer its foal's high trumpet-like cries with deep, growling sounds. Stallions have the ability to produce additional sound utterances: they can grunt, squeal and downright screech. Stallions make grunting sounds when they are trying to attract a mare and as a prelude to mating. To our ears their squealing and screeching sounds imperious and aggressive, and that is no doubt the intention. When stallions want to impress one another, they arch their necks, touch each other on the nose and scratch, all the while stamping the ground violently with one of their forelegs and at the same time holding their heads high

Right: Things can become quite overheated between stallions.

and squealing loudly. These encounters serve as a mutual demonstration of rank and usually take place peacefully.

Demonstrations of rank frequently end with a pile of faeces: one of the two participants sniffs at a pile of old dung which is lying around, steps over it and makes another pile. The two horses then sniff this pile intensely. Only the dominant one of the two will dare to be the last one, in the presence of the other horse, to leave its faeces on top of it. If the inferior horse accepts the claim, it will then walk away. The sequence of the faeces piles is not as important if both animals are undisputed family stallions. Depending on the situation, such as whose mares are just making their way to the drinking trough, one of the stallions will move away first, without waiting for the other one to deposit its faeces or doing it itself. After all, the horses know each other and each is aware that the other has the same status as a family head as it does. These encounters become more serious when a young stallion is involved. It is too young to possess any mares and so all the family stallions see it as a rival. A

fight can break out if the younger horse fails to recognise the superiority of the older one and tries to be the last one to leave its faeces. It is not rare for a stallion to react to situations like this with a shriek, indicating its extreme agitation.

Horses have a very highly developed sense of smell. Old and new droppings in an area always attract the attention of the stallions. By smelling it they are able to determine which stallion or mare made the pile. In any event, family stallions scent-mark the droppings of their mares, and only these, with their own urine. The droppings of mares in heat are the object of especially intense sniffing and are frequently urinated upon by the stallions. Afterwards the stallions frequently fleer, bearing their upper incisors, which means that they stick their heads and necks up and purse their lips until their nostrils are almost closed. What this does is open up the olfractory organ which is located at the end of the nasal cavity. This organ helps horses to distinguish the slightest nuances of smell. They also need this organ when they come across a smell they are not familiar with and want

Left: Horses can see well, especially at a far distance, and have excellent hearing. They also use their ears to indicate their moods.

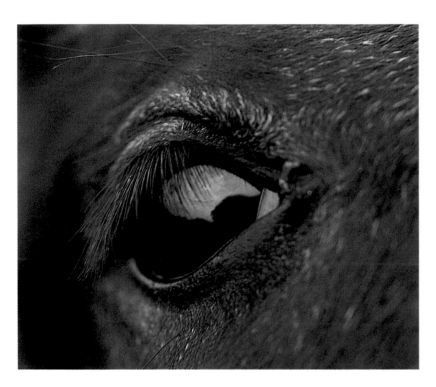

The eyes of horses are not constructed like those of humans. Through certain movements of the head, horses are able to focus their eyes sharply to different distances.

to investigate, such as the smell of tobacco or a new kind of feed. The horse's keen sense of smell apparently also allows it to locate water, which could be a long distance away.

Horses have just as hearty a yawn as humans do and this is sometimes wrongly interpreted as laughing. However, they do not yawn when they are especially tired but instead as they start waking up after a long rest or when leaving the rolling ground. Probably as a form of relaxation stallions yawn heartily after lovemaking or after clashes with their rivals.

Sight and colour perception

In all probability horses are colour blind. If anything, a horse will probably notice a blue sky because the rods in its retina, which are responsible for detecting colour, are sensitive to tones of blue. The horse has far more of these than of the rods which react to red tones. The reason why the poles in show jumping are painted in red and white is because these visibly

contrasting colours produce a pattern which horses can easily distinguish from the rest of the background. But even the most vibrant colours are no guarantee that a horse approaching with its head down will see an obstacle in time or see it clearly. This has to do with the construction and function of their sight organs. Like so many other vertebrates horses have eyes which are capable of focusing so that the image projected by the retina is equally sharp whether seen from a distance or from close up. However, horses' eyes have a different way of focusing from afar to close up. Their eyes are unable to alter the shape of the lens (in any event not as much as we can) in order to focus from distance to close up because the muscles required for this movement are not well developed. Horses make up for this deficiency by raising or lowering their heads or moving their eyes. This action allows an object to be sharply focused on a certain part of the retina. On the one hand, objects which are located close by are visible in the upper half of the retina; on the other hand, those which are far away are visible in the middle. Because the horse's eyeball is not evenly round but slightly flattened out, there is a variance in the gap between the lens and the retina. To see an obstacle sharply with both eyes from a medium to far distance, horses try to raise their heads.

To make matters worse, right before they reach an obstacle they are let down by their normal two-eyed way of seeing. They will then turn their heads so they can judge the situation clearly using one eye only. Riders in show jumping often use a martingale with a strap which is usually adjusted too tightly to force the horse's head downwards, thus denying it the freedom of movement it needs before the jump to make its own assessment of the obstacle. The horse has no other choice than to trust its rider to signal the jump at the right moment. This is the same reason why horses try to lower their heads when they are stepping over poles on the ground. It is the only way they can even see the poles and avoid stumbling.

As inadequate as they might be for a ride through a forest of poles in show jumping, the eyes of a horse are excellent for the survival of an animal grazing in a field. Horses' eyes are among the largest in the animal kingdom. The field of vision of a horse's eyes overlaps at an angle of 60-70 degrees at the front so that it can see from both sides and three-dimensionally. The combination of eyes that are positioned at the side of the head, and a rather large retina, means that horses have the ability to see a large sweep of their surroundings.

The only thing horses cannot see when holding their heads in a normal position is what is right in back or immediately in

A rustling noise can cause sudden fright, because during their development horses have learned to react immediately and 'in a panic' to signs of danger.

66 front of them. But a slight turning of the head is all that is needed to bring these blind spots into their field of vision. The horse's ability to see during twilight hours and at night is far superior to ours. However, their sensitivity to light is at the expense of their capability to distinguish clearly. Horses see more than we do, albeit less sharply. Stationary objects are more difficult to distinguish than moving objects; the explanation given for this is that the horse's retina has a large number of nerve cells which only react to the stimulus of motion. During the course of time, however, this has proven to be an advantage; it helps in the early detection of predators sneaking up on them.

Even if horses cannot recognise exactly what is approaching them, they have learned to take flight immediately rather than to put their lives at stake by hesitating. The only weapon the horse has against its enemies is its speed during flight. With its rigid back, highly developed hocks,

nostrils which are capable of enlarging to provide for a larger intake of air and an excellent blood supply to the muscle apparatus, it is well-armed for it.

The only remaining predators of horses living in the wild are pumas and wolves. If a stallion sees something strange appearing on the horizon, it throws up its head and snorts. This alarms the other members of its family grouped behind it. If the source of the disturbance turns out to be serious, the horses run off and stop again after about 50-100 metres/165-328 ft. With their nostrils flaring they attempt to pick up the scent of the supposed enemy. But they adapt their speed according to the degree of danger in the situation. At a walk or a trot they avoid objects which are still at a distance. This way they are not wasting any energy on threatening situations which could prove to be harmless after the fact. However, if they are caught by surprise in their immediate area, they will suddenly flee at a gallop.

Friendship can develop between horses and humans, but this will not happen overnight, and even then it is only possible if the animal has accepted the person as a superior member of the group. **Opposite below:** Lato follows behind Monika on the field as a sign of his friendship, although he actually would like to be eating some grass. **Above and above right:** He loves to play tricks on her, or greet her with a gentle nudge of the nose. **Centre right and below right:** Bandola also snuggles up to Kim at every opportunity, and Saga is obviously comfortable with the caresses he gets from Nina.

BREEDS AND BREEDING

The ancient Greeks, or even one of the earlier civilisations such as the Egyptians, were the first to practise selective breeding to achieve certain characteristics in horses, rather than allow them to reproduce at will. Early breeders would have selected mares and above all stallions that appealed to them especially as particularly fast or strong animals, or as animals with other characteristics they valued.

Through selective breeding, a total of around three hundred different breeds of the domestic horse developed in the course of many centuries. The achievements of some of the horse breeders are without doubt impressive, and nothing should be said to detract from this in any way. But it is a widely-known fact that the basis for the large variety of breeds was created by nature before humans intervened.

Domestic horses originated from different types of wild horses.

A war over horses

Very early on, in about 500 BC, the Persians made a deliberate effort to breed dappled horses. This led to a year-long war with the Chinese. The Chinese emperor Wu Ti (126 BC) offered the Persians a large amount of gold in exchange for a breeding stock of dappled horses, but the Persians refused his offer. These dappled horses were considered sacred and were reserved for the Persian king and his royal household. Angered, Wu Ti sent his troops off to get what he wanted by force, but by the time these warriors finally brought back a small number of dappled horses, 40,000 men and 100,000 horses had been killed. This serves as an example of the stupidity of wars.

Selective breeding

Wild animals are exposed to all sorts of dangers: predators, the cold, sweltering heat, lack of food and other adversities claim their victims. Weak and sickly animals have little or no chance of survival. So it is only when healthy, strong and hardy animals survive to reproduce that the stock of an animal species will remain healthy and capable of coping with life. Moreover, with horses, only a relatively small number of stallions – those which are particularly strong, self-assured and intelligent – have a chance to conquer a herd of mares and to protect it in battle against jealous rivals. In this way only the best ones are able to pass their qualities on to their offspring. If they start to lose their strength they are forced to make way for a younger horse. Nature has its way of selective breeding just as clever breeders do.

Landscape, climate and availability of food also play their part in selective breeding. The more extreme the living conditions are, the more the animals have to specialise and adapt. That is why a small, stocky horse with particularly sharp teeth

and a generous rump, large enough to accommodate efficient digestive organs, evolved in the marshlands and glaciers of the north. These characteristics also enabled it to feed on tough stems and leaves, tree bark and other fibrous materials. This horse's thick oily coat protected it well against the cold and damp weather and the plague of insects in the summer. So today the ponies of the north, the Icelandics, Shetlands, Exmoor and Dartmoor ponies, are not animals that have been bred by humans, but are descended from the prehistoric wild ponies. Even today they possess some of the characteristics of their forefathers, even if they have been altered in some way by human efforts to breed in them desirable traits.

The desert areas in southwestern Asia also form an extreme living environment. The wild horses that once lived there had a totally different set of problems with which to contend. They were easy to spot in the open countryside and always had to be ready to take flight in a flash. They had a delicate build which was geared to speed, and an explosive temper and an alertness to potential danger. As can be seen in numerous reliefs and wall paintings, the Egyptians and Assyrians had horses of this desert type, which served as the basis for the later breeding of the incomparable Arabian thoroughbred 300-400 years ago.

The numerous horses that lived in the enormous steppes of eastern Europe and Asia and in the forests of Europe were exposed to far less harsh conditions. They also needed speed and stamina because they were one of the main prey of wolves. Otherwise they did not require any special traits. Three forms of this type of horse are still known today because they did not die out until fairly recent times: the last forest tarpan died in the 18th century, the last steppe tarpan in the 19th century. They

Above: The Haflinger, a small Austrian horse still used by farmers in the Tyrol.

were probably the most important ancestors of our domestic horse. The third one in the group, Przewalski's horse, also almost died out. A systematic breeding programme was developed on the basis of a few dozen specimens of this last true wild horse found in different zoos. Nevertheless there are about 200 Przewalski's horses in existence again today.

Thoroughbreds

There are only two breeds in the world that are allowed to be described as thoroughbred horses: the pure-bred Arabian horse and the English thoroughbred. Of the two, the Arab is the most important horse in the history of horse breeding. To many people it personifies the most beautiful and perfect horse of all.

Many legends surround the origins of the breed. In all probability its ancestors were delicate, swift primeval wild horses of the desert which were able to run as fast as lightning. What was important in the further development of the Arab was the brilliant understanding of horses by the prophet Mohammed. In his sacred writings, the Koran, he gave instructions and rules on the breeding of Arabian horses. For centuries horse breeding had been in the hands of the Bedouins who lived in the highlands of Arabia. To them the only thing that mattered was performance: toughness, speed, endurance, an unde-manding nature and submissiveness to the point of total exhaustion. Only animals possessing these qualities were used for reproduction, and the breeders attached a great deal of importance to preserving the purity of the different lineages.

Beginning around the 14th century horse traders all over the world started searching for, selling and exporting Arabian horses. Most of the other thor-oughbreds in the world as well as many of the heavy horses and pony breeds were improved through interbreeding with Arabs. Above all this cross-breeding made them livelier, easier to ride, faster and tougher, but also much more docile. Other prominent characteristics of the Arabian horse include a remarkably friendly person-ality, intelligence, a good disposition towards humans and a special ability to learn, features which also played a role in the origins of the English thoroughbred.

The English thoroughbred

Some 700 years ago the English were already pairing off pony stallions and mares which had proven themselves in racing, breeding them for speed and endurance. It is no wonder that the Arab stallions which were brought into the country in greater numbers from the 15th century onwards were much sought after for covering the native pony mares.

Top: Exmoor ponies are almost perfectly preserved wild prehistoric ponies. **Above:** Wild white horses of the Camargue are adapted to hot summers but can also cope with cold winters. **Overleaf:** Arab horses running wild in the Namib desert.

Actual thoroughbred breeding in England began around 1700. The female basis was provided by some 24 pony mares, which apparently all had a large amount of Arab blood in their veins. A total of 103 Arab stallions are listed in the English *General Stud Book*, but amazingly all but three of

The first progenitor of the Arab was a wild desert horse which also was a very fast and slender animal. We know from numerous sources that the Assyrians and the Egyptians were breeding horses similar to the Arab as early as 3000 to 4000 years ago. Today Arabs are bred all over the world.
Above: A pure-bred Arab in Switzerland.
Right: Two Arabs in New Mexico, USA.

these stallion lineages have died out. All the English thoroughbreds in the world – today there are about one million – originate from these three stallions. As was customary at the time, they carry the names of their owners: Byerley Turk, Darley Arabian and Godolphin Bard.

Captain Byerley was with the English army when the English helped to liberate the city of Vienna from the Turks in 1683. At this time he came across a light-brown stallion which, like so many of the horses belonging to the Turks, was extremely well-trained and possibly a true Arabian. The

captain rode this horse for another seven years and then Byerley Turk was taken to a stud farm in England. While it did not cover that many mares there were some excellent animals among its descendants. Above all its great-great-grandson King Herod, which was born in 1758, became one of the greatest studs on record in thoroughbred history.

The story of Darley Arabian is quite unspectacular. It was supposedly given to Thomas Darley in Syrian exchange for a rifle. Thomas sent the beautiful pure-bred horse to his brother Richard, where the stallion covered mares until it reached the ripe old age of 30. Among its many excellent descendants its great-grandson Eclipse was the most important. Eclipse was born on 1 April 1764 during a solar eclipse, hence the name. Because of its very difficult temperament the breeders wanted to castrate it but then decided against it. Eclipse ran in 18 races and always won effortlessly without needing any goading by its jockey. But, most importantly, it passed on its qualities with incredible success. Today over 90 per cent of all English thoroughbreds descend from its bloodline.

The influence of Godolphin Barb on thoroughbred breeding is considerably less significant but its history is all the more remarkable. It was a Berber horse with a great deal of Arabian blood and had a perfect build, although with its massive fat neck and tiny ears it would have been laughed out of a contest for the best-looking horse. An aristocrat from Tunisia

Left: The Arab thoroughbred is considered by many to be the finest and most beautiful of all horse breeds.

presented the horse as a gift to the French King Louis XV (1710-74). Sham, as the horse was still called then, apparently did not appeal at all to the ruler and was made to leave the royal stables. It is said that the horse was then used to pull a water cart through the streets of Paris but this appears to be a legend. In any event, the horse was bought by an Englishman called Edward Coke in 1729 and, following Coke's death, was left to the coffeehouse owner Roger Williams, who in turn sold it to Lord Godolphin. At the lord's stud farm it was

Above: There is no doubt that the Arab is the most important breed of horse, mainly because it was used all over the world to refine many of the other horse and pony breeds and because it was the basis for the breeding of the English thoroughbred.

apparently first used as a teaser. A mare which is to be covered is often first led to this kind of test stud. Her reactions show whether she is ready for mating. If this is the case, the mare that is to be covered is brought to the actual stud and the teaser is left to look on.

Fortunately for Godolphin Barb and thoroughbred breeding the mare Roxane one day stubbornly refused to have anything to do with the stud horse. For better or for worse the breeders replaced it with the test stud. The fruit of this mating was Lath, a superb top-class horse. Later, Godolphin Barb covered numerous other mares and produced some very excellent offspring before it died at the age of 29 on Christmas Day in the year 1753.

Without doubt, the English thorough-bred is the best racing horse for medium distances. However, many thoroughbreds are also very good show jumping or event-ing horses. But what is important is that the thoroughbred has greatly refined and improved many other breeds. Modern race-horse breeding would be inconceivable without the English thoroughbred.

Types of horse breed

The large majority of domestic horse breeds can be divided into three main groups: ponies, heavy or work horses, and thor-oughbreds and other horses used for sport-ing and recreational purposes. In the horse show and sporting arena, horses which stand less than 148 centimetres high are generally labelled ponies. This is quite logical. However the zoologist sees it quite differently. To the zoologist ponies are those small horses which descend from the prehistoric wild ponies and have at least some of their characteristics. The confusion caused by the varying uses of the word 'pony' can be seen from the following examples. On the one hand, an Arab is

Above: Most fans of horse racing would agree that the English thoroughbred is the undisputed king of the racing track.

anything but a pony, although a good many of these horses are less than 148 cm/59 in high and thus are in the pony category. On the other hand, the Icelandic is a perfect specimen of a pony from the standpoint of size, type and characteristics. However most enthusiasts of the Icelandic firmly insist that others call this animal a horse, as if there were something .inferior about being labelled a 'pony.'

As recently as the first half of the 20th century muscle-packed heavy horses were still playing an important role as draught animals. However, within a short period of time mechanisation in farming, industry and transportation made them superfluous. The stock of these animals in some coun-tries shrank by more than 90 per cent. Only some of the lighter breeds which were more versatile, such as the Haflinger, Freiberger and Fjord horses, succeeded in surviving and actually even increased in number. However, coming across a massive Belgian, Clydesdale or Percheron is quite a rare event these days anywhere in Europe.

By far most of the horses that are bred today are sporting horses. All horses aside from ponies and heavy horses belong to this group, including the thoroughbreds. There are approximately three hundred breeds of these horses, and in earlier times they came in many different varieties. However during the last few decades most of the animals in this group have been bred with a specific purpose in mind. The first priority is given to riding horses which are suitable for dressage and show jumping. The result of this notion of an ideal modern horse is that hardly anyone can tell the difference today between a Swedish horse and an Anglo-Norman or an Italian racehorse. Therefore a colourful range of different breeds has evolved into a standard European horse.

Western Horses

As recently as the 1970s, Western horses were still almost solely restricted to North and South America, but they are now becoming increasingly popular in parts of Europe. Although it is basically possible to ride Western saddle with any kind of horse, the different types of the American Western horse are particularly well-suited to this kind of riding. The various types of Western horse are described below.

MUSTANG

The wild mustangs of the western United States are not wild horses but descendants of the Spanish horses which returned to the wild after they were brought over during the conquest and colonisation of America. They multiplied in the millions on the prairies and shared the grazing land with large herds of bison. Just like the Indian buffalo most of them were later slaughtered, but thousands of them were also caught and trained for use as cowboy and cavalry horses. Many of the horses used by cowboys today are direct descendants of the mustang. There are many different types, varying in height from 130-148 cm/52-59 in. All of them are known for their toughness, undemanding nature and endurance.

Above: The breeding of sporting horses would be inconceivable today without the English thoroughbred. Breeding of thoroughbred horses began in England as long ago as 1700.

PINTO

The name Pinto comes from the Spanish pintado and means painted. Long ago many of the Spanish horses were dappled, as were the mustangs later. Thus as a rule pintos are mustangs or descendants of these wild horses. There have been deliberate attempts since 1963 to raise them as a breed. Animals with just the right conformation and of course dappling are selected for this purpose. Depending on their markings there is either the predominantly dark Overo or the mostly white Tobiano. Like the other ancestors of the mustang, pintos are on average less than 150 cm tall; they are fast, have stamina and are extremely robust. They are excellent cowboy and domestic horses.

APPALOOSA

The Indians were always particularly fond of spotted horses, but apparently it was only

The solid, heavy-boned prehistoric wild horses of the north, the so-called tundra horses, formed the basis for the breeding of heavy horses, some of which are shown here.
Right: The heavy, predominatly dapple-grey Percheron, which can weigh up to 1000kg, originated in the Le Perche region in France.
Below right: The impressive Clydesdale comes from the River Clyde area of Scotland.

the Nez Perce tribe in Idaho which systematically bred horses and valued speed, toughness and attractive markings. In 1877 the Nez Perce tribe was defeated by the US cavalry after having been chased mercilessly for a month. Their horses were confiscated. Fortunately there were people who recognised the quality of the animals and carefully continued breeding them. The Appaloosas with their different kinds of spotted markings and excellent qualities for riding are an enrichment to warmblood horse breeding. The fact that there are well over 150,000 of them in existence today proves how popular they have become. A number of excellent Appaloosas can also be found now in Europe.

QUARTER HORSE
The Quarter horse is not a quarter of a horse as the name would imply. It is also not a thoroughbred, as some people claim,

Left: The relatively lightweight and agile Freiberger from the Swiss Jura is still actively being bred as a work and recreational horse; it is particularly suitable as a draught horse. **Below left:** At a live weight of about 800 kg, the French Ardennais is one of the medium-weight heavy duty horses. As with most others of this type, the stock of this horse has dwindled considerably during the last few years.

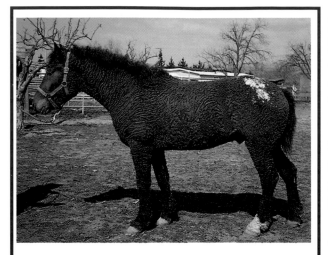

Bashkir Curly

The Bashkir Curly is not only covered in curls but also surrounded by legends. This horse, which stands 150 cm/60 in high, is powerful but also light and agile and stands out because of its unusual coat. Its long hair forms tight curls on its entire body, almost like the coat of a poodle. This horse is only bred by a few enthusiasts in the United States, who claim that their horses descend from the Bashkir pony which has been bred for many years in the southern Ural mountain area. This could be possible, although no one knows how these ponies could have come to America. Nevertheless, the Bashkir Curly remains a remarkable horse.

but nevertheless it has earned its place on a high pedestal. These horses made a reputation for themselves about 350 years ago in the American South and not in the Wild West. In the southern states horse racing on the village streets was popular entertainment on Sundays. The races usually ran for a distance of a quarter of a mile (about 400 meters) and this is how its name Quarter horse originated.

All sorts of different breeds of horses were crossed to create the Quarter horse – a large number of Arabian and English thoroughbreds as well as Turkish horses and others. What was important in the stud

Above: The Swedish sporting horse, a noble riding horse capable of high standards of performance in sport, something that is much in demand today. **Opposite above:** During the 17th century the Andalucian from southern Spain played an important role in the breeding of parade horses. **Opposite:** The influence of the fine Trakener breed is obvious in this Würtemmberg .

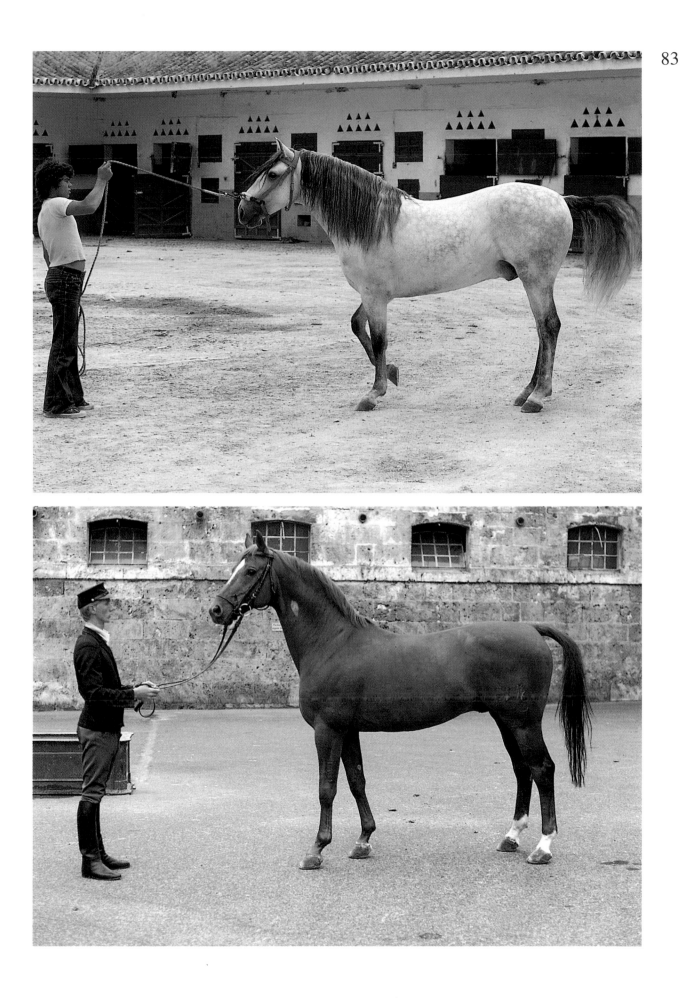

Thanks to their contentedness, hardiness and lovng natures as well as to their incredible abilities, ponies have been enjoying an increase in popularity for decades. Some of the important breeds are pictured here. **Right:** an Icelandic. **Centre left:** a Norwegian Fjord pony. **Centre right:** a Shetland pony. **Below:** A modern version of the Dartmoor.

Below: The Macedonian mountain horse, a tough horse the size of a pony, is actively being bred, especially in Switzerland, and has proven to be a very good recreational horse. **Bottom:** The very noble Welsh ponies, which are bred in different sizes and types, are among the best-loved ponies in the world.

Record Weights

The photograph above is of Nero, a Belgian heavy horse from the Hürlimann Brewery in Zurich weighing 800 kg/1600 lb. At nine years of age the Belgian mare Wilma du Bos, born on 15 July 1966, weighed in at an incredible 1088 kg/23,900 lb. However a stallion of the same breed called Brooklyn Supreme outdid the heavyweight Wilma by a long shot: before it died in 1948 at the age of 20, it weighed 1440 kilos. There is no doubt that this animal was grossly obese.

The English shire horses are considered to be the largest horses in the world. The height of the stallions is frequently almost 2 metres/6½ in. Two shire geldings, which together pulled a combined weight of 51 tonnes at a competition, are celebrated as the strongest horses in the world. The smallest horses are the Argentinean Falabella ponies. The very smallest one of this breed was born on 8 February 1978 in the United States and given the name Tung Dynasty. It stood 30.4 cm/12 in high at the withers.

The Twitch

The twitch consists of a loop of rope which is placed on the front part of the nostrils and pulled. In earlier times people spoke about 'distractive pain,', which means that they believed that it was possible to distract a horse from something unpleasant through the pain caused to its nostrils. We have become wiser since then: numerous fine nerves are located in the horse's top lip. When this area is pressed together through a twitch it apparently activates the release of certain substances in the brain, which are known as endorphins. These reduce the sensitivity to pain and cause a type of trance – in a way the horses experiences a 'high' If it is used properly the twitch is a sensible device, for example when the horse is being treated for a painful injury

selection was that the animals were able to thunder from one end of town to the other in record speed.

At its inception, the American Quarter Horse Association (AQHA), which was not founded until 1940, set itself the goal of producing a breed which totally fits its ideal of what a Quarter horse should be.

It sought a solid, muscular but refined-looking horse with a short, wide, expressive head and wiry, very robust legs; a quick learner, friendly and competitive; a horse which was high-spirited but not nervous.

The versatility and quality of the Quarter horse is shown in its success as a stud horse. During the association's first year 599 horses were listed in the stud book. Today more than three million Quarter horses are registered at the association's American head office in Texas. Today these animals can be found world wide in 64 different countries.

From foal to horse

It is amazing how horses mate under natural conditions. For weeks there is a strong air of excitement within the herd. The stallion is constantly on its guard, trotting around its mares and protecting them jealously from its rivals. In most cases it has to deal with the appearance of a young stallion which is still on its own but is already feeling strong enough to capture its own harem. Making a great fuss, arching its neck upward to make it look even larger and stronger than it is, the younger horse attempts to intimidate its rival but does not always succeed. Then the horses engage in a violent fight until the stronger of the two has proven itself.

It is during this time of the year that the mares give birth to their foals. About ten days after giving birth they go into heat, which means that there is a period of about five to eight days during which they can become impregnated, and because of this

Western horses in Europe.
Left: 'Horse of Geronimo', a first-class Appaloosa stallion, in Germany. **Below:** The excellent Quarter horse mare 'Dales Altra' with her one-week old son 'Taco Domingo', in Switzerland.

they are prepared to mate with a stallion. So a stallion, using its reliable instinct and led by its sharp sense of smell, must go around to each mare to find out when the time is right for mating. It spends all of its time trying to woo one or the other of its mares. With a spring in its trot it delicately dances around them, its neck arched and tail raised, as though it were well aware of how splendid it looks. Again and again it approaches the chosen mare, sniffs at it and 'pinches' it affectionately with its teeth until the female horse is ready for coition.

The complicated mating ritual is as much part of a horse's life as is eating and drinking. And the result is that when horses breed in the wild, more than 90 per cent of covered mares become impreg-nated. In contrast, only about 50-60 per cent of mares that mate in captivity become impregnated.

Horse breeders are generally reluctant to allow their mares to mate as they would do in the wild. This is because they feel that there is a greater danger of injury to the stallion during the act of free mating. Admittedly it is possible that a mare which is not ready for mating and is being pestered by a stallion could kick out and scratch the stallion. However if the mare's horseshoes have been removed beforehand the danger of serious injury is extremely minimal.

There are a large number of breeders who for years have been allowing their stallions and the mares to be covered to run freely in the fields during the mating season

88 and have only had good experiences doing so. Almost every mare has become pregnant and moreover all the animals, the mares and the stallion, are so obviously more contented and more balanced; consequently they are friendlier to people. This actually is totally logical.

People are always trying to outwit nature, although in doing so they almost always cause something to go wrong in the long run. Many horse breeders not only prevent natural mating behaviour, but very often also disregard the natural mating time as well. The English began this as long ago as 1823. Because the natural time for foals to be born coincided with the beginning of the flat racing season, the English Jockey Club – the association which also controls the breeding of thoroughbreds – postponed the time of birth to early January. Stallions are mainly procreative all year round and mares can usually mate every three weeks if they are not carrying. Although their fertility is reduced during the winter months, it can be helped along: heating the stalls, lengthening the days by using electric lights and using high-energy feed to fake the quality of spring grass all work to increase fertility. The mares are then covered towards the end of January and give birth to their foals about 340 days later, during the first part of January of the following year.

The foals must spend the first few months of their lives in a stall, and so it is no wonder that so many foals do not develop properly and are frequently sickly and need the vet. Dust from the stalls and the smell of ammonia are damaging to their health and they lack proper exercise and the high-energy spring grass.

In nature the mating period lasts from March to the end of August. With horses which live in the wild or in wild preserves practically all the mares are impregnated during this period. When the foals are born a good eleven months later it is the warm season of the year and new grass is available in abundance – the best food for them and for nursing mares. Grazing in the meadow is also important exercise for the foals. The young animals must be given the chance to romp around as much as possible. This is the only way that their bones, muscles, tendons and all their internal organs can develop properly. And this is the only way they can grow into healthy horses.

Young stallions practising a playful duel – but with full-grown stallions this type of behavior can end up being a bloody, serious matter.

Raising foals

For many breeds, including ponies, shows and auctions of foals are held in the autumn. In order to ensure that the foals are as large as possible by then, the mares are often already covered in February. So

even with other breeds the foals have to spend months in a stall before they are finally allowed to rollick around in the fields.

Foals are among the most delightful creatures imaginable, and many horse owners are tempted by this into thinking about raising foals themselves. But before making this splendid idea a reality and starting to look for a stud for your mare there are a number of things you have to think about.

Above all, breeding means taking responsibility. You should not venture to take this step until a number of conditions have been met. The first thing that is required is extensive practical experience

Two stallions fighting for the right to mate with the herd mares. Raising themselves up on their hind legs they lash out at each other with their teeth and hooves. The battle will continue until one of them recognizes the superiority of the other and flees.

Left: In nature, exhibitionism is part of the mating ritual of horses. **Below:** During the first few weeks of its life, a foal will develop a very close bond with its mother. Later on, it gradually seeks contact with other horses of of about the same age.

Horses

Horses everywhere are divided into three types based on sex. As one can see, a stallion is without doubt the male horse. A mare is the female horse. A gelding is born as a stallion. However stallions are easier to control if they lose their masculinity, and they do not keep causing a commotion as a result of the constant to-do with the female horses. If the reproductive organs are removed the horse will become indifferent toward mares.

Above: Mare and foal stay together constantly during the foal's first few weeks of life. The foal depends on its mother not only for food but also for protection and the invaluable lessons it will learn from her about living in a herd.
Below: In the wild, a foal born during the spring will be living an independent life by the time autumn arrives.

Below and right: As happens with wild horses, the covering period for domesticated mares should always be planned so that the foals are born in spring and are therefore able to be outdoors as much as possible from the moment of birth onwards. This ensures the healthy development of a horse.

with horses. Only then is it possible to monitor the well-being of mares and foals. Moreover a foal should never grow up on its own. It should be able to romp about and play with other young horses of the same age. This is not only important for its physical development but also for its social behaviour. As a general rule foals which are raised on their own turn into problematic horses.

Foals also need a lot of pasture land. Pregnant as well as nursing mares and foals should be able to graze for at least twelve hours a day.

Finally, breeding does not simply mean producing horses. Only mares with the right conformation and disposition which have been examined by the breeding commission (vetted) should be covered, and of course only a perfect stud which has also been

vetted should be used for this purpose.

If you cannot meet these conditions then it would be better to leave the breeding to someone else. After all, it is altogether possible that you will have another chance to think about breeding horses later in life. And if breeding is carried out within the right framework and under the necessary conditions you will enjoy the experience even more.

FEEDING

During the course of its development, the horse had to adapt to the changing conditions of its environment. The transformation from a leaf-eater to a grass-eater, together with the transformation into a solid-hoofed animal, was probably the most important step in the evolution of the horse. Grass is a considerably tougher food than leaves and buds because it contains silica fibres. The horse is only able to cope with a diet of grass because its molars gradually widened, and a hard dental cementum was deposited in the ridges of the enamel. The latter protected the teeth from excessive wear. In addition the large intestine expanded to accommodate the digestion of quantities of fibre-rich materials.

The food available to horses during the early days of their domestication fluctuated according to the season of the year, as it did for their wild ancestors. It was not yet usual to have dried grass or leaves available for bridging the winter months. The breeding and maintaining of a large number of horses in stables (it is said that King Solomon kept 12,000 riding horses and 4000 carriage horses as early as 3000 years ago) and the amount of hard work this entailed forced changes in foodstuff and in feeding techniques. A horse could no longer cover its increasing energy needs through grazing alone; even additional grazing time would not have made enough of a difference. The problem was solved with the transition from a nomadic existence to an agricultural one in the second century BC, because now the horse owner had feed in the form of high-energy grain which the animals could eat in less time. In addition to barley, which was mainly used in southern Europe for animal feed, horses in northern regions were given oats, rye, wheat, millet, spelt and peas. The favourite horses of the emperor Caligula were even spoiled with raisins, almonds and honey. And indeed one of them was even made a senator.

The horse's taste in food has not changed much since its domestication. Short meals of two to four hours in length interrupted by one to two-hour resting periods correspond to the natural rhythm of freely living horses responsible for finding their own food. Depending on the quality of the food available, horses spend 12-16 hours a day grazing, whereby the time spent eating and resting is equally distributed over daytime and nighttime. Only when the insects plague them too much during the day do they eat more at night. In these circumstances they search for a windy and barren spot, huddle close together, roll in the dirt or rub up against each other and with their tails whisk the pests away from each other's head. In addition to grass and plants horses living free also like to munch on leaves and bark from willows and aspen as well as blackberries. They use their hooves to scrape away the snow in the fields and they do not seem to mind frozen grass. They are not even afraid of marshes: standing up to their stomachs in water and sometimes with their nostrils half submerged, they eat the tasty reeds.

Horses use their very pliable lips and their tongues to bring the grass into their mouths and their front teeth to bite it off almost down to the ground. Harder substances, such as turnips and apples, are first chewed into little pieces with their incisors. Horses are very fussy eaters. If they do not like something or they are not familiar with it, they will leave it lying on the ground. They grind up their food using

Opposite: As well as feeding on grasses, horses also like to nibble on bushes and trees. **Above:** Horses need water – in fact around 25 to 30 litres a day. **Overleaf:** A barren field with many different types of plants is the best place for horses to graze.

their molars. When they chew their food it is reduced into very little pieces and mixed with saliva, making it soft so the horse can swallow it.

At the end of its gullet in the stomach there is a strong muscle which automatically contracts when the stomach is full; this is why horses which have overeaten cannot vomit. Their stomachs are relatively small and look like a bean. The gastric juices, which in the lower membranes contain pepsin and hydrochloric acid, break up the albumen in food and supply it to the body. The stomach of horses is a particularly sensitive organ. Its contents must be saturated with sufficient gastric juice before they can be digested properly. Too much activity after eating, too much food at once or eating too quickly prevent this from happening and can lead to an excessive build-up of gas or to excessive fermentation.

In the attached small intestine sugar, albumen, starches and fats are broken down by the enzymes secreted by the pancreas and the mucous membranes of the small intestine, and are absorbed into the lining of the intestine. Two-thirds of the proteins from grass and grain and around one-third of the total of all digestible food is processed in the small intestine. Anything which cannot be digested in the small intestine is returned to the adjacent large intestine. This part of the intestine consists of several multi-chambered sections. In the appendix and in a large part of the colon carbohydrates such as the cellulose in straw and hay are broken down by bacteria and unicellular small organisms, the protozoans. This takes time. During the process of digestion, 85 per cent of the activity takes place in this section of the body.

In the last section of the digestive tract, in the colon and in the rectum, the indigestible left-overs become thickened

98 through dehydration. It is the colon with its small indentations that gives the faeces its characteristic apple-type form. On average a horse discharges its bowels every 30-90 minutes. The frequency and the amount vary according to the type of food eaten, its water content, how much activity the horse has had, and so on. The fact that young foals eat the faeces of their mothers is very sensible: it provides the young horses with essential B vitamins and helps to prevent protozoans settling in their intestines.

The more efficiently the food elements are absorbed before reaching the large intestine, the more efficiently the energy provided by nourishment is assimilated into the system. How much of its food can a horse even use? It benefits the most from turnips and grains: up to 85 per cent of the amount it eats is digested and provides energy to the body. Horses derive the least benefit from straw, of which only 35 per cent can be broken down. As a general rule: the more raw fibre content food has, the less digestible it is. Oats, barley and maize are rich in protein and are the most common feed for horses. Even while the horse is still chewing, the valuable substances contained in the seeds are squeezed out and digested in the stomach and small intestine. Because oats are large and have a high amount of husk, they must be chewed well, and they should be mashed frequently to make them easier for the horse to digest. It is best to crush barleycorn or grind it coarsely, as it is very hard and horses often swallow it whole without chewing it because it is so small. Maize is easier to digest than oats and consequently is higher in energy; it is mainly fed to high-performing horses. Wheat and rye are less suitable because they stick together in the

stomach and therefore can cause serious health problems.

Concentrated foodstuff should be fed in small quantities. In tune with the natural rhythm of their bodies horses generally need to be fed frequently and only in small quantities. In earlier times work horses had their first feeding by five o'clock in the morning, and their fourth meal late in the evening. Even though this kind of feeding frequency is no longer feasible in most places, it should be stressed that long intervals between feeding have an unfavourable effect on the health and performance of a horse. The stomach-intestine channel is overloaded if too much feed is made available all at once, and as a result not enough steady nourishment is supplied to the decomposing micro-organisms, which effectively reduces their number and ability to function. If horses are only to be fed two or three times a day, they should not be required to engage in any activity for 30-60 minutes after they have eaten. A full stomach will restrict their breathing and reduce their efficiency.

In addition to nourishment the horse is also dependent on roughage and structural substances. So-called bulk food such as straw and hay is plant material which is rich in raw fibre. It regulates the amount and speed of food ingestion, forces the horse to chew and to salivate, stimulates the bowels and is essential for activating the intestinal flora. With every feeding it is beneficial to give a horse the bulk food first and then about 15 minutes later to add the fortified feed. This helps the process of salivation of the latter and causes it to pass through the stomach more slowly.

With too little roughage a horse's molars do not grind down evenly and this leads to excessive fermentation caused by an insufficient production of saliva, bad habits caused by lack of activity, a general lack of nutrients because of an unsatisfactory synthesis of the intestinal bacteria and constipation because the bowels are not working hard enough. Therefore the raw fibre content in feed should not amount to less than 16-18 per cent of the total ration. Converted, this means that each horse

Opposite: High, tall-growing grass and hay is easier for horses to digest than fresh spring grass, which is high in protein.
Right: A welcome change for every horse in winter — grasss that has been scraped out from underneath the snow.

From left to right: Rye, winter wheat, summer wheat and barley.

should be given at least 2 kg/1 lb of hay or straw per 100 kg/110 lb of live weight each day. Straw provides little protein but has a high raw fibre content. The most nutritional types of straw are the leafy ones such as oat straw. The type which is used most and also is easy to digest is stalky wheat and barley straw. As far as storage and quality are concerned, straw is similar to hay.

Hay is and has always been the most important feed for horses because it not only has all the qualities of good roughage but half of it is also digestible. A horse should be fed good quality hay, meaning that it should be fresh and look green. Pale hay is a sign that it was harvested too late, was too wet or was stored too long. Brown-looking hay has superheated during storage and hay which feels damp is still too wet. During the first few weeks of storage hay sweats. Shortly after harvesting germination begins inside a pile of hay. The water which forms in the process combines with the hot air in the bale and forces through, condensing on the edges of the outer layers. The germination does not stop until the water content reaches about 15 per cent. The hay should not be used for feeding until this process has been completed. It also should not smell musty or foul; this could be the result of a dangerous mould.

Ponies and small horses are not different from large horses in the type of feed they are given. However smaller horses require proportionately more energy for their metabolism than do large horses. Because they have a larger surface area in relationship to their live mass they emit more heat to their surroundings. This applies to ponies from warmer climates with part-thoroughbred or Arabian blood such as the New Forest pony, the Welsh pony or the Haflinger. However, ponies such as the Shetlands, Icelandics or Fjords, which for centuries were bred in areas where the ground was barren and have adapted to being kept in open conditions, should be given ten per cent less feed in comparison to their weight. Because of their heavy coats and the thick fat tissues in the deeper

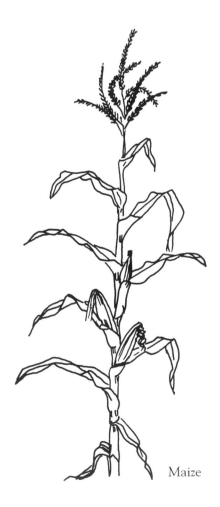

Maize

Oats

The less digestible feed is, the more excrement a horse produces and the more water it needs to drink. With 10-20 kg/22.44 lbs of excrement per day between 7.5-15 litres/13-26 pints of water is passed. Water is also important for regulating a horse's temperature. During heavy exertion and in high outdoor temperatures horses lose up to 7 kg/15 lb of sweat per 100 kg/220 lb of weight. To compensate for this loss of fluid horses must drink more. They prefer clear, fresh water but outdoors they often must make do with brackish, polluted or even salty water.

part of the dermis they emit less heat to their surroundings and have a quiet temperament.

Small horses eat considerably more slowly than large ones. They have a smaller masticating surface and consequently less space for squeezing in larger particles. Large horses require about 40 minutes to chew and swallow a 1 kg/2 lb bale of hay; small horses, on the other hand, need twice as long and for oat kernels and food in cubes they even need four times as much time. Irrespective of size, all horses in open stables need additional food during the winter as soon as temperatures reach -10°C to make up for heat loss. The best thing to give them is hay because the animal will benefit from the warmth produced in the large intestine.

If a horse is only fed hay and oats or gets its nourishment only from grazing, it frequently will not obtain enough of the mineral substance sodium. Salt licks help to make up for this deficiency. Artificially-produced provender is being used more and more frequently. The advantage of this mixture is that it provides a balanced diet, it is easy to handle and it usually contains suitable amounts of different vitamins and minerals as a supplement.

Beware of Poisonous Plants!

The warning to be on the look-out for poisonous plants must be taken seriously, but there is no need to examine each square meter of the meadow for little plants with toxic properties or to pull them out. Poisonous plants are not very tasty and most horses avoid them instinctively. In the field they simply ignore plants such as these, including the buttercup, the marsh horsetail and St John's wort. However it is dangerous for horses to remain in fields which have been grazed and consequently may have nothing left on them but these plants.

Horses which are not given enough to eat, are tied up outdoors and are bored, are also apt to pick at some poisonous plants. The effect of noxious plants vary. For example, St John's wort is less harmful to them than most, causing sunburn on non-pigmented skin, while buttercups affect the mucous membranes in the mouth, causing infection and colic, followed by diarrhoea and a general condition of weakness. In the dried state when it is mixed in with hay and straw the buttercup loses its toxin and is no longer poisonous.

However, do watch out for plants which are still poisonous even when they are mixed in with hay. These include the horsetail, bracken, Adonis eye and meadow saffron (illustration 6). For example, if hay mixed with meadow saffron is fed to horses over a period of several months it will cause hypersensitivity, muscle spasms and difficulty in walking.

You and your horse may also come across dangerous plants when riding in a

1

2

3

forest or a park. Yew (illustration 7) is one of the most toxic and has an immediate effect. A small amount, for example only 100 g/3 ½ oz of yew needles can prove fatal to a horse.

For the benefit of your horse you should also be on the look-out for robinia (illustration 5), especially its bark. If a horse eats any of this, it starts to sweat, goes into convulsion and can die within a day. The same fate awaits animals which have eaten buds or seeds from the laburnum (illustration 1) or leaves from the box tree (illustration 3).

You must also take care with the water hemlock (8) which grows in marshes and swamps. All it takes is a piece of root the size of a walnut to kill a horse. Other plants that are dangerous for horses are oak (illustration 2), meadow saffron, lupin, common beech (illustration 4) and water dropwort.

To a large degree the effects of poisoning depend on which part of a plant (bark, leaves, buds, fruit) has been eaten and how much. Some of the more dangerous types of plants are illustrated. Will you recognise them again if you come across them in the open countryside?

If you suspect that a horse has been poisoned by a plant, you should immediately call a vet to the scene. A vet sometimes can still prevent further disaster from happening.

As a preventive measure it is recommended that horses should never be left to stand next to hedges of yew or any other potentially dangerous bushes, and that plants such as these should be totally removed from areas where horses are regularly apt to be tied up or exercised. But as stated earlier, it would be foolish for anyone to look into a horse's mouth with fear each time it has eaten something green while out on a ride.

Keeping horses always means restricting their movements. Horses are by nature inhabitants of wide open spaces, living in groups for which contact with other horses is vital. They exercise, they almost constantly keep on the move looking for water and food and are ready to take flight at any time.

All these needs arc totally ignored in traditional stabling. Since the Middle Ages at the latest and until a few decades ago it was common to tie up horses in their stalls. Almost without exception these were work or military horses, which were being used

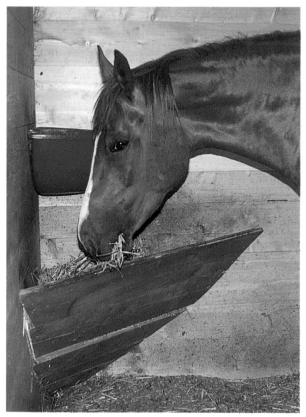

Above: In the wild, a horse bends its neck and head while it is eating. In the stable, mangers should therefore be positioned sufficiently low to allow the horse to feed naturally.
Opposite: Even for Arabs, access to fresh air year in and year out is the best thing for them.

practically every day and often from early morning to late at night. Their life was hard, but at least these horses were never bored. Their natural urge for activity was satisfied and body contact with neighbouring horses was possible, even though it was restricted. Animals which were kept in this manner rarely developed any bad habits in the stables.

In some cases horses are still being kept like this today, particularly in some riding stables. Many people do not even give this a second thought, but it is not the correct way to keep a horse.

The practice of keeping a horse in a box is not any better. Such boxes are cages with bars running up all the way over the top, in which horses are locked up, with no possibility of any body contact with the horses next to them. These animals often do not have more than one hour a day outdoors for exercise or they are only required on weekends if the weather is good. In addition, their owners often think that their horses are well looked after, although they may not be. Such owners may wonder why their horse suddenly becomes quirky, develops bad habits, becomes less friendly and finally even starts to bite or kick. This type of unpleasant or even dangerous behaviour is seldom an inherent character trait; it almost always develops because a horse is either not being kept in the proper conditions or is not being handled correctly. Of course horses can generally be said to be difficult or easy, but by nature they are never vicious.

Boxes are only acceptable if they are large enough (a minimum of 3.5 metres/ 11½square ft) and are open at the top so that the horses can sniff and nibble each

other over the top of the box. But even when horses are kept in this kind of facility they require some diversion for at least a few hours a day: grazing in a field, work or exercise in a paddock, or, if possible, allow a little bit of everything. Even better is a group enclosure, such as a large stable, in which at least two horses can move freely about at the same time.

The best way to keep horses is in an open stable with as large an exercise area as possible. There still seems to be a general view that only the more robust breeds should be kept in open stables. This is incorrect. In many countries horses and ponies of all different kinds of breed live outdoors year in and year out. Even some pure-bred Arabs may live in an open stable

Stuffy air in a stall can cause
serious respiratory ailments. In
summer and in winter, horses
should have a lot of fresh air —
the cold does not harm horses
kept in open stables.

Disturbed Behaviour

The expression bad habits in the stable is often used, although it is misleading. Behavioural disturbance would be more appropriate, meaning undesirable habits which develop out of boredom. The fault is not with the horses themselves but with the incorrect way in which people keep them. These bad habits are almost unknown with horses which are kept in groups but occur frequently with individual horses kept in boxes. The following are a few examples. The horse stands with its front legs slightly apart and swings its head back and forth, sometimes for hours on end (weaving), or swallows air by pulling back its larynx as it tenses its neck muscles (roaring), causing an uneven build-up of gas in its stomach, which may develop into digestive problems and colic. The horse may paw the ground and hit the wall, resulting in injury to its legs, or use its teeth to work over objects it finds in its box (grating), which damages its teeth. Other disturbing behaviour in horses caused by poor stabling includes sticking out the tongue, refusing to lie down, shying away, and showing nasty reactions.

Some remedies for such behaviour include straps to control roaring, electric fencing in boxes, muzzles, even operations in which the muscles in the neck are cut to prevent the horse from swallowing air. The best way to deal with bad behaviour in the stable is to eliminate the cause, and that means providing proper living conditions for the horses.

Below: If a horse is in a box facing the outside instead of in an open stable, then it should at least be able to look out all year round – even if it is only a little Shelty. **Bottom:** It is unfortunate that some horses have to be tied to exercise machines such as this one because they spend the rest of the time standing in narrow stalls. Only fresh air and proper exercise produce a contented horse.

all year long and in spite of this will be fit and contented. Every horse can adapt to this way of life. Of course a horse should never be taken from a warm stable and put into an open stable in the middle of winter. Even if healthy horses are able to develop a thick coat in an amazingly short amount of time, when there has been a sudden drop in temperature they must have a chance in early autumn, at the latest, to adapt to living outdoors.

Autumn is the time when horses more or less develop a thick winter coat. Some ponies even look like they have been dressed in bearskin. For many people this is

108 an important reason for locking the horses up in closed stables and possibly even covering them up. Naturally horses with a thick coat will quickly start to sweat if they have to do any kind of work. But in most cases it should be possible to ride the horse more sparingly in the winter and to have it walk the last half hour of the ride, something that should be done anyway. A horse should never be left sweating, neither in a stable nor outdoors.

If it is not possible to have an open stable, then it is a good idea to leave windows and doors open day and night, so that there is no draught, summer and winter. Horses which are kept in conditions like this develop a high level of resistance, mainly against coughs and sneezes. The cold will not harm any horse which is used to it, but the ammonia vapours which accumulate in closed stables can lead to dangerous chronic illnesses.

The Stud Farm

There are many different types of studs. Probably the oldest type is the wild stud, in which a herd of mares is kept with one

Below: Le Pin, the French state stud farm. **Centre:** The main German stud farm in Marbach. **Bottom:** The Spanish private stud farm Cortijo de Quarto. **Opposite right:** A trotter stud farm, Hanover Shoe Farms in the United States. **Opposite below:** Childwick Bury, the thoroughbred stud in England.

selected stud in a large nature preserve for the whole year or during the mating season. The Dülmen wild horses in Nordrhein-Westfalia in Germany, for example, live in this kind of semi-wild stud. Many ponies are still being bred in wild studs today where they are left to their own devices. Once a year the young animals are caught and removed, usually when they are about six to twelve months old. The surplus male foals and the female foals not suitable for breeding are usually sold at auction. With this form of stud there is a very high rate of impregnation: as a rule more than 90 per cent of the mares become pregnant. Under other stud conditions the rate of impregnation is often only around 60 per cent.

A national stud farm is a state-run institution that controls local horse breeding. In a sense this is a kind of depot where the local stud horses are kept. During the mating season some of these stallions are distributed to individual stud farms and made available to private breeders. The breeders can come to such places to have their mares covered by good studs for a relatively small stud fee. In this way a country can promote local horse breeding. In some countries there are also state-run central studs, with first class stud horses, prime mares and stallions, which are used for breeding the stallions for the national stud farms, and private studs where mares (but not necessarily stallions) are kept.

GROOMING

A horse should be groomed before each ride or, if for some reason this cannot be done, then at least every two days. But it would be wrong for a horse which lives in an open stable or spends a great deal of time outdoors to be brushed until it shines every day. By doing so, you remove too much of the oil from the horse's hair so that the coat is no longer waterproof and the rain is able to penetrate through to the skin, and that means the horse may be in danger of catching a cold. So always use moderation when grooming your horse.

Use a coarse brush or a rubber comb to remove the heavy dirt and encrusted sweat from the horse's coat. Also use a brush and comb daily to brush out the loose winter hairs from the coat during the shedding period in spring. You are thereby doing your part to help the animal to deal with this strenuous process. Take a softer hairbrush or currycomb to brush out the dust and scurf from its coat, mane and tail.

If the horse's legs are dirty, clean them using a wet cleaning brush or, what is even easier, spray them with a hose. Incidentally, after you have been riding and especially after a strenuous ride you should use the jet of a water hose to cool off the horse's legs, particularly around the pasterns. In summery temperatures, hose down the whole horse after riding; even if you are not able to ride, give it a shower every day, but don't use shampoo because that would thoroughly remove the water-repellent oils from its coat. You can use a towel to give the coat an additional sheen.

One of the most important grooming tools is a hoof pick, which is used to scratch out the dirt and grit from the horse's hooves before riding. After riding and at least once a day you should examine your horse's hooves for stones or other small objects. Horseshoes are particularly liable to collect objects that are able to lodge themselves in the hooves and cause pain.

Left: The cleaning box with a brush for cleaning the hooves and a hoof pick (top); a rubber curry comb, a metal curry comb, a body brush and a coarse dandy brush (left to right bottom).
Right: The rubber curry comb is used to remove dry mud (top), the soft body brush (below) to remove dust and scurf from a horse's coat.

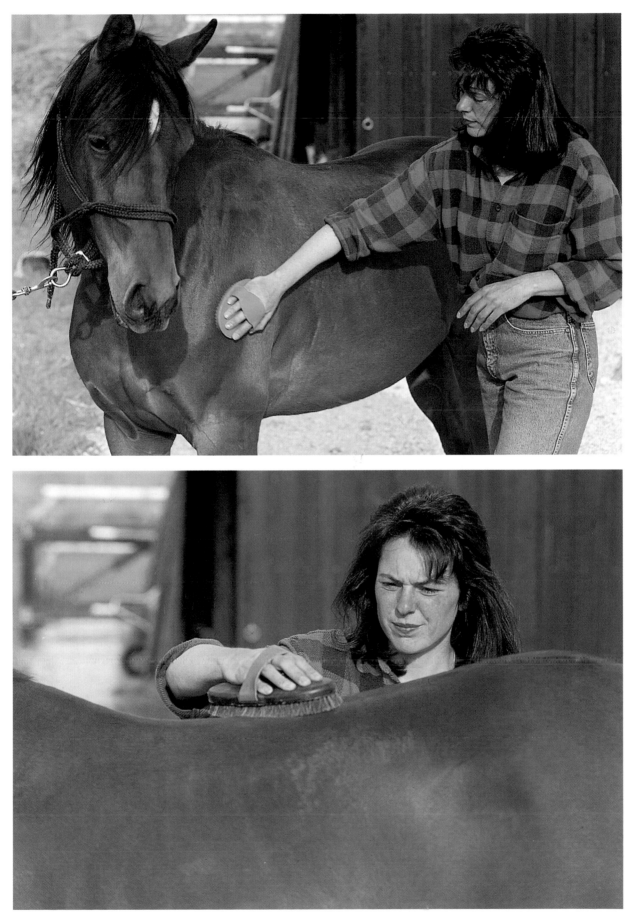

If you want to, you can oil the hooves to make them shine before an event, but it is better not to, because hooves must be able to absorb moisture to keep them healthy. Brittle or cracked hooves should not be oiled either but should be kept as moist as possible. The best way to care for your horse's hooves is to massage the rim of the coronet of the hoof daily using bayleaf oil or a bayleaf oil hoof salve.

Grooming means more than just keeping your horse clean; it also means body contact. You have probably already noticed that horses sometimes nibble each other, mainly around the withers area. They mainly touch each other on the parts

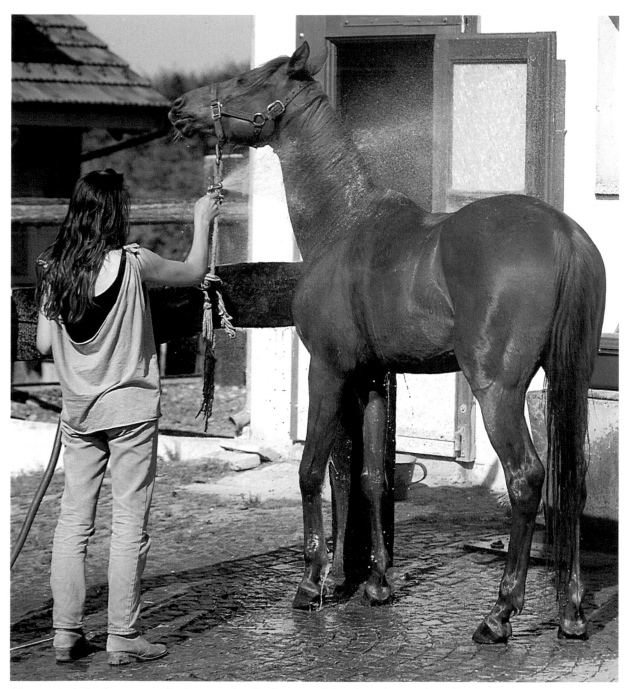

Above: A daily shower is refreshing – for the horse and for the rider. **Right:** The feet should be thoroughly cleaned out before and after riding to remove dirt and stones.

If you want your horse to look particularly smart for a special occasion there is nothing wrong with creative plaiting – but please do not cut off any part of the horse's hair.

of their bodies which they cannot reach themselves. When they nibble each other they also show that they like and trust one another. Behavioural scientists call this activity social personal hygiene. The same applies to grooming. You rid the horse of dirt, of itchy residue on the skin, of shedded hair. You show it that you are its friend and gradually build up a strong relationship of mutual trust.

Because horses clean each other, young horses in particular also want to nibble people. But because this proof of affection is not really good for the delicate skin of humans, you must make the horse stop this behaviour. Even if you happen to be wearing a thick jacket which would provide some protection from the horse's nibbling, you should still always give the horse a little tap on the nose until it understands that people are not to be cleaned. The same applies when horses beg and then start nibbling. If you are not consistent in stopping this behaviour the nibbling can easily

develop into painful biting. For this reason it is wise not to give your horse a treat at every opportunity. This is actually teaching it to beg.

The best approach is to reward a horse with a sugar cube when it has done something well, learned something new, left the field as soon as it was called, and so on, and even then do not give it something every time. Feeding from the hand should not become a habit and you should not use treats to bribe a horse, only to reward it.

Coat, Mane and Tail

Just as hair adorns human heads, the coat, mane and tail form the natural embellishment of a horse. But of course nature does not allow a horse's hair to grow for the sake of appearance but to fulfil certain important functions.

The hair on a horse's body repels water, so protecting it from hypothermia. This does not happen simply because the hair is constantly being lubricated by the glands in the skin to make it water-repellent but also because of the way in which it grows. The direction of the growth runs from the back towards the stomach; this is why water runs downwards like it does from tiles which are layered one on top of the other on a roof. Different cowlicks function as shunts on a railroad and divert the water. For example, the cowlick on the horse's hip bone directs the water coming from its back to the stomach and to the outer side of its thighs. It protects the almost hairless inner sides of the horse's thighs from getting wet. The forelock and the mane help the water from the rain to run down the horse's head and crest. The tail prevents the anal area from becoming wet. In actual fact it is mainly the short hairs growing at the side of the dock which are very important – they are not called top hair for nothing. The fetlock hair protects the almost hairless area above the hoof, the hollow of the heel, not only from the wet but also from injury from branches, stones, frozen snow, and so on. The horse's thick winter coat with its coarse oily hair and soft hair underneath provides important protection against the cold.

Hair also has an important function for warding off insects. The horses use their tails to chase irritating pests away from their bodies and with their forelocks they keep the insects away from their eyes. Insects usually have a difficult time penetrating into the ears of a horse because of the numerous fine hairs that normally grow in that area.

The long hair on the chin and around the horse's mouth has a totally different function. This hair is connected to the cells governing the sense of touch. A horse's eyes are, in the main, very effective for seeing into the far distance, but they can barely distinguish things which are right under its head; however for this they can use their tactile hairs.

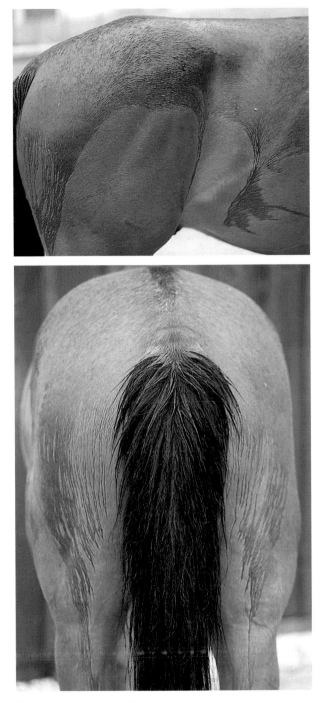

Here you see how effectively the horse's hair repels water from the rain. Although many owners cut off some of the top hair from the side of the tail this is totally absurd, as this hair provides important protection. Snipping it off will not add to the attractiveness of the horse.

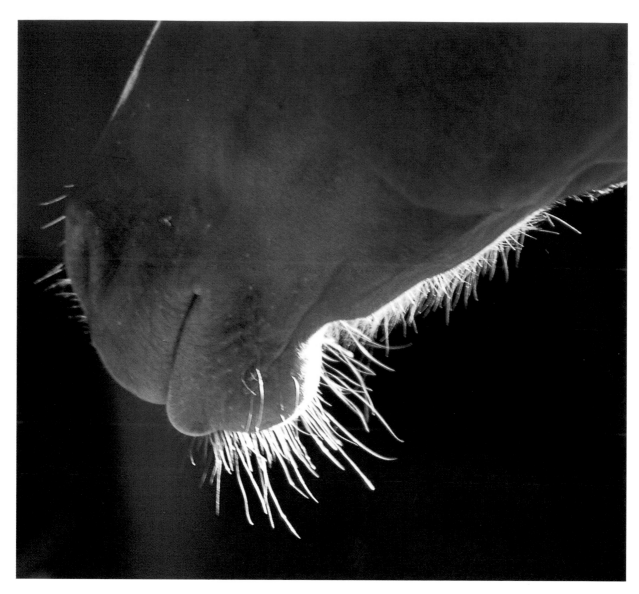

116

Please no shaving! Fine hairs such as these around the horse's chin may appear to some owners to be of no importance, or even unsightly, but they are there for a very good reason. They are part of the horse's tactile organs and relate to the sense of touch, enabling the horse to feel and react to changes in its environment.

In this way nature came up with all sorts of ideas for improving the horse's lot. And what do we do? Until a few years ago it was customary to cut the tail of work horses very short. Animal protection laws prohibit this practice in most countries, but it is still being done here and there. Otherwise you can snip around your horse's tail as much as you want to. Some widespread absurd practices include docking a horse's tail, trimming away the hair from a horse's ears and removing all the hair from the pasterns. Many horses have their manes trimmed and

Left: Why do some owners insist on cutting the manes of Fjord ponies? Their natural appearance, complete with shaggy mane, is very appealing. Cutting off the mane is a frivolous fashion.

Right: This Tennessee Walking Horse has been radically shorn of all the hair on its head. Below right: In some cases dark make-up is still being applied to the eyes and nostrils of Arabs when they are being shown, regardless of any harm this may do the horse or how foolish it makes it look.

their forelocks cut off because it is a tradition. Whether this is more attractive than a flowing mane is a matter of taste, but in any case it is wrong to remove an animal's natural protection and it unfortunately proves that there are still many people who have little understanding for their horses. And that is not all: on some horses the tactile hairs on the chin and nostrils are shaved off. This must be as bad for a horse as it would be if you lost the sense of touch in the tips of your fingers.

As far as different ways of walking are concerned, humans have very few options available to them. Whether they walk, jog or sprint, they always alternate between putting the right foot and then the left foot on the ground. A horse with its four legs has many more combinations available to it.

Every horse is born with the ability to do three different gaits: the walk, the trot and the gallop. With the normal walk the foot sequence is right fore foot, left hind foot, left fore and right hind, sounding like an irregular four-beat. With the trot the sequence is right fore and left hind (at the same time); left fore and right hind (at the same time); it sounds like a two-step. In a canter (left gallop) the horse puts down the left fore, right hind, then the left hind and right fore simultaneously; so you can hear three thuds at an even rhythm followed by a short pause during the period of suspension. In the right canter the sequence begins right fore. This is not at all as complicated as it seems. Try to imitate these gaits using all four of your limbs.

Some horses are also born with an inherent additional gait: the pacing gait. This ability appears in horses more frequently than you might think. It is even a typical characteristic of certain breeds, such as the Paso horses and the Icelandic ponies. In the pacing gait the hooves do not set down diagonally as they do in the trot (crosswise) but diametrically (counter crosswise). Thus: right fore and right hind (at the same time); then left fore and left hind (at the same time). You can also easily imitate the pacing gait using your hands and feet.

Horses which are pacers also have the ability to tolt. The tolt can be characterised as a variation between a pacing gait and a normal walk using very fast steps. A well-executed tolt sounds like a pure four-step. You very probably will fail if you try to imitate it using all fours.

The distinctive feature of the tolt is that the rider is trotting forward at a fast pace without being shaken about. He or she sits firmly in the saddle and simply floats along. This is why pacers used to be very desirable but since the growth in popularity of the military style of riding during the last century "five-gait" horses were no longer in demand. Yet in certain remote areas of the world, such as in Iceland, Peru and Colombia, there was an appreciation for the comfort of the tolt and consequently

The walk: right fore foot, left hind foot, left fore foot, right hind foot – all at a more or less comfortable, four-beat gait.

Top: The trot consists of moving the right fore foot and the left hind foot simultaneously. It sounds like a two-beat gait and is not particularly comfortable, either for the rider or for the horse. A slow, easy canter (Western riders call this a lope) would actually be much more comfortable for both parties.
Left: The gallop – the fastest gait of all. For the rider, this is almost like flying.

horses with a fine natural ability for the different kinds of gaits were specially bred.

During the last few decades more and more riders in other parts of the world have taken an interest in these multi-gaited horses. The most popular ones are the Icelandic ponies. which have helped in reintroducing the tolt. In more recent years, the fiery high-bred Paso horses from South America have been in evidence in Europe and North America.

120 Icelandic Ponies

When the first Icelandic ponies appeared here 20 or 30 years ago, most riders looked down on them with a sympathetic smile. However the small horses soon exhibited their many fine qualities. They became a symbol of a totally new approach to the horse, a symbol of recreational riding, and evoked a new attitude towards horses living in rough outdoor conditions and the proper treatment of them. Today there are around 2500 Icelandic ponies in Switzerland alone and almost ten times that number in Germany.

Characteristic of these hardy horses from the north is a very expressive and usually short pony with a wide forehead, large eyes and small furry ears which almost disappear into a heavy mane and thick fore-

A specialised gait: an Icelandic pony at tolt.

lock. The neck is more likely to be short and heavy, the body strong and sturdy, the legs short and wiry. Standing still, Icelandics look like calmness itself. But as soon as they are saddled, they become lively and full of energy, and outdoors in the open they display the kind of sure-footedness and endurance one only dreams about with large horses. They almost always have a lovable nature, even if they often have a mind of their own and need strict training.

In spite of their small size (on average they are about 130 cm/150 in tall) Icelandics are able to carry large adults with no effort. Impressive proof of just what these small horses with a big heart are capable of was provided at the so-called 'largest horse race of all time', a competition organised to mark the bicentennary in the United States that ran over a distance of 600 km from New York to California. Among the approximately two hundred horses taking part there were 14 Icelandic ponies, which no one gave the slightest chance of reaching the goal. Almost half of all the horses dropped out early because of exhaustion or leg injuries. But all the Icelandics made it to the finishing post.

It is through these loveable horses that we have again learned to appreciate the pacing and tölting, or racking, gaits. The pace is a gait in which the horse moves its legs together in pairs, using the two legs on the same side of the body. They rhythm of the gait is 1-2-1-2-1-2-1-2.

In the tölt, or rack, the pony moves its legs as in the pace (moving two legs on the same side) but 'breaks' the pace so that one leg moves just after the other one. The rhythm here is a tapping, four-beat sound: 1-2-3-4-1-2-3-4.

For years now competitions with horses performing the different types of gaits have been held in Europe and North America.

Paso Horses

The Icelandics had firmly established themselves in Central Europe by the time the Paso, a totally different kind of pacer, was introduced from South America.

In general appearance the Paso horse is a particularly fine-looking breed. It descends from Spanish horses with a large percentage of Eastern blood, which were brought to South America after about 1500. The Spanish settlers who stayed after the Conquest looked for horses which had endurance, were sure-footed and afforded maximum comfort when riding long distances. At the same time the horse was also an object of prestige among the proud estate owners: it was a status symbol and was used to show the prosperity and wealth of a person. In addition the horses were required to have an undemanding nature, the right height (about 150 cm/160 in), a friendly, willing and loyal disposition as well as a lively temperament.

Paso horses have a very special, fiery aura. They have a noble, fine head with clear eyes. A flowing mane covers the powerful, upright neck. Their bodies are muscular and nicely rounded; their legs are slender and wiry.

The best-known Paso breeds came from the Andes; namely the Peruvian Paso in Peru and the Paso Fino in Colombia.

The first Paso horses were imported to North America in around 1960 and within a very short period of time attracted a large number of fans. In 1973 the first Peruvian Pasos and Paso Finos were taken to Switzerland, and a short time later they appeared in other European countries where they became very popular.

Pasos make excellent family and recreational horses. And anyone who has sporting ambitions and enjoys the different gaits can participate with their horses in competitions such as cross-country, dressage and trail riding.

Fiery pacers from Colombia: Paso Finos.

Is it Natural?

Sports activities such as Western and long-distance riding, along with competitive games on horseback and events involving going through the paces, are becoming more and more popular. There are many horse lovers who look for sports that are more suitable to the horse's character and capabilities. Of course what some might refer to as an enjoyable horse sport, others might consider pure horse slavery. For example, in the United States the Tennessee Walking Horse Association practise a special type of display gaits that are shown in contests at fancy horse shows. In the particularly popular 'running walk' the horse lifts its knees (actually it is the carpal joints in its forelegs) very high off the ground. It reaches so far forward with its hind feet that its croup drops down sharply and it looks as if the back part of the animal's body will collapse at any moment. A whole range of offensive and nasty tricks are used to teach a horse how to perform gaits such as this.

First the front feet are weighed down with wedge-shaped rubber blocks which are progressively increased in size so that they can be up to 12 cm/4 ½ in high on a horse ready for competition. The angle of the hoof and the weight are changed according to the type of gait required.

Another practice is to place loose chains around the horse's front pasterns, which hit the sensitive coronet each time the horse takes a step. The pain this produces causes the horse to lift its feet even faster and higher. For greater effect sharp chemicals are often applied to the coronet to make it even sorer. A high, or 'nicked,' tail is another effect frequently sought. This is achieved by cutting through the dock muscle which normally pulls the tail downwards and then shortly before a showing spreading a sharp ginger ointment into the anus. It comes as no surprise anymore that even the true instruments of torture like curb bits and spurs are included in the range of hair-raising methods.

Vaulting – gymnastics on the back of a horse

Vaulting is the name given to gymnastic exercises performed on a galloping horse: it teaches physical control, promotes balance and develops self-confidence. Actually every new rider should be advised to begin vaulting as soon as possible. On the lunge, without a saddle or reins, the beginner learns how to achieve a good seat on a horse without the use of one's hands. No one, not even adult riders, should claim that this is not important. For years the head trainer at the Spanish Riding School in Vienna has been training his pupils on the lunge. Whether you are satisfied just doing the easy exercises or you also want to attempt some of the more difficult ones, either way it is a lot of fun! For exercising on horseback you need a horse which has been well trained on the lunge. It is fitted with a special girth which you can use to hold on to and a cavesson to which the lunge and side reins are attached and has bandages to protect its legs.

Before each vaulting lesson the horse is warmed up by being exercised on the lunge without the use of side reins or a rider. The rider should also do some warm-up exercises to loosen muscles, tendons and joints. The first exercises are done with the horse at a walk: try to grab the horse's neck with both your arms, touch the horse's ears with your hand, lie on the horse's back or touch your toes with your hand. If you enjoy this kind of activity, why not ask your riding instructor to show you how to do the exercises known as the flag, the round-the-world and the flank. All these become more difficult when done at a trot. It will take practice and more practice before you feel

secure and supple enough to stretch your arms to the side or to cross them. You should not attempt any other exercises while riding at a trot. This gait is too fast for settling into the movements; it also provides too little momentum for gymnastic exercises. A lot of things are easier when done at a canter: the powerful movements of the horse give you the momentum you need for mounting and dismounting and for other exercises.

Sporting fun on a turning horse: vaulting.

Riding as a form of Therapy

For some time now ponies and horses have been used for therapy and for sport with people who are physically disabled or mentally handicapped. The animals best suited for this purpose are those which are balanced and calm, have strong nerves, an excellent disposition and are well-trained. This kind of riding does not merely entail taking children or adults out for a ride on the back of a horse.

For example, when used to help patients loosen up tense muscles or increase the mobility in their spinal column, a horse must walk carefully without deviating from its gait and take even steps. When it is being mounted, the horse should also remain very still and not lose its head, because the rider may frequently be stiff and sit uneasily; it should respond to softly spoken commands and set out or stop gently. All of this demands the horse's fullest attention: it must react to the person leading it as well as to the helper.

Contact with horses can also have a positive affect on the spirit and psyche of a person. Therefore a great deal of time is dedicated to caring for and leading horses which are ridden for therapy. It is not training an individual how to ride that is paramount but rather the encouragement it gives them. For a disabled child or a young person this can mean building a relationship of trust; for someone else it can mean training and co-ordinating one's own movements to coincide with those of the horse, such as leading the horse through an obstacle course. It is always enjoyable for both parties and lots of fun.

Riding Reins

Riding reins make it easier to train both horse and rider. Their purpose is to clarify and reinforce the rider's aids for the horse; but they are not designed to help awkward riders to get a better grip on their horses. The reins should be used with common sense. Any forced exercise in which the long run causes resistance in a horse will lead to failure. The use of aids on horses should be evaluated on an individual basis to determine whether or not they promote an understanding between the horse and the rider.

Side reins are a popular aid for replacing the rider's hand. They allow beginners to focus on keeping their balance and achieving a good seat without causing any irritation to the horse's mouth. Side reins are fastened to the left and right of a lunging or saddle girth and in front to a cavesson or snaffle rings. The right length of the side reins can only be roughly estimated before a rider is seated; usually they must be shortened or lengthened during the work session depending on the horse's gait. Side reins should not be fastened at the beginning of the work or at the end so that the horse first has a chance to move freely about and get rid of any stiffness.

A standing martingale has the same effect as normal side reins with the added advantage that it also allows a horse to stretch. It passes from the saddle girth between the front legs through to the chin girth where it is firmly fastened.

Draw reins are ideal for lunging young horses which have not yet been trained,

The side rein (illustrated right) is used to replace the rider's hand, for example when lunging and vaulting. The standing martingale (illustration below) works in a similar way, but gives the horse more freedom.

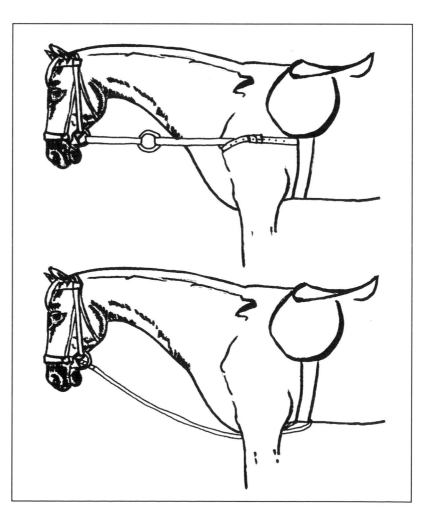

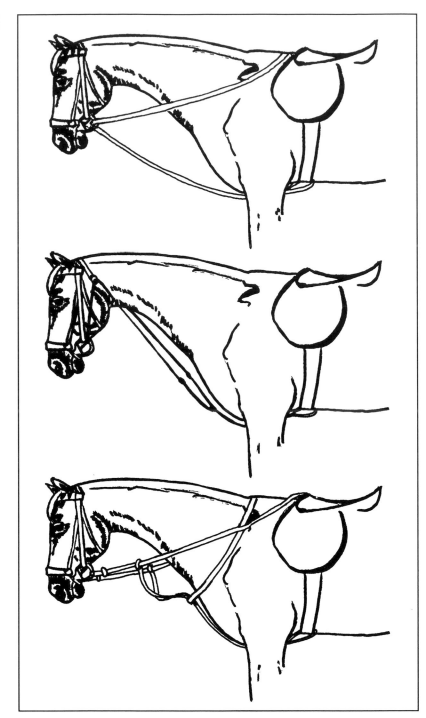

The draw rein (top) is a good aid for lunging young horses. The chambon (centre) is used for lunging horses which stick their noses forward and hollow their backs. The running martingale (bottom) should only be used on a limited basis with horses which toss up their heads when they are being ridden.

because they do not overly restrict the horse's movement like the side reins do, but instead indicate forward-backward direction. For lunging the draw reins pass from the bottom of the saddle or lunge girth between the forelegs of the horse and up through the snaffle rings; they are then fastened at the top of the saddle or lunge girth. As the reins are not firmly fastened to the snaffle rings the horse is not hindered when it wants to extend or stretch itself. This rein can also be used for riding, but only by a skilled rider who has the sensitivity to relax the reins at the right moment.

Horses that point their noses forward, hollow their backs and do not bring their legs underneath their bodies enough when they are worked on the lunge can be taught the right way with the help of a chambon. When the horse is not relaxed this puts pressure on the occipital bone, located immediately behind the ears.

The running martingale, an adjustable strap that passes through the forelegs of a horse, should not be necessary on a well-trained animal. It is not allowed in dressage tests because of the assumption that the rider will never require a martingale to make up for his ineffective use of the reins in controlling the upward movement of the horse's neck and head. If for some reason the horse tosses up its neck and head, any manipulation of the reins will put pressure on the mouth opening and molars and thus become ineffective. The actual purpose of this particular rein in a situation such as this is to establish a contact between the rider's hand and the horse's lower jaw. Under no circumstances should you use a martingale to rein down the head of a horse for any length of time. In most cases a restless neck and head is the result of a lack of strength in the hindquarters combined with the poor seat of the rider.

Below: There is no need to use a martingale with a well-trained horse. It appears to be part of the normal equipment of these three riders – but then something else appears to be wrong here as well.

It is not difficult to mount a friendly, well-trained horse and allow yourself to be carried about at a walk. But this does not have a great deal to do with riding except that you are sitting on a horse. Riding is an art. It requires solid training as well as a capacity for understanding and some natural talent. Without a pinch of talent you can take a hundred riding lessons and still never become a good rider. On the one hand, talent consists of a good feeling for the movements of a horse and, on the other hand, the ability to think like a horse.

Good riders exist everywhere – be it the Bedouins in the Arabian highlands, the herdsmen in Mongolia or the gentlemen riders in a dressage rectangle – even if they all ride differently. The difference lies not only in the clothing and the saddling but also in the style of riding.

There is still a widespread opinion in Europe that the European or English style is the only correct and cultivated form of riding. This is not so. In any event, during the last few years there has been a growing awareness that other techniques also exist.

The European style originated with the ancient Greeks and is well documented in the works of Xenophon, Greek historian and soldier. During the Renaissance this style was refined even further by various well-known riding instructors such as Grisone and Pluvinel (see pages 38-40). This classical style of riding was the basis for the current European style of riding. It

Above: English-style dressage. **Overleaf:** Western riding.

originated in the manège and even today is best suited to the manège.

A Spanish herdsman would not have derived much benefit from training by a Pluvinel or a Cavendish. His horse was not required to impress but rather to function and that meant carrying out its work out in the countryside. As early as 1000 years ago the Vaqueros had their own style as well as saddles and bridles suitable for the kind of work they did. Incidentally, the Romans had similar riding methods and saddles. The Spanish conquerors and colonists brought along their horses, their saddles and their riding style to South and Central America and then to California. From there the Vaquero method also spread to the cattle herders in the North American West. As time went by the Spanish saddles and bridles were somewhat modified - and this is how the Western saddle came into being. The cowboys then tinkered with the riding style of the Vaqueros and the result was Western style. This style is currently making quite a name for itself on the European riding scene.

If someone dresses up like John Wayne, swings a Western saddle over his Freiberger (Swiss horse) and gallops wildly through the countryside, this by no means makes him a Western rider. Above all many beginners make the big mistake of inserting a curb bit into the horse's mouth. A curb bit should only be used with horses which have largely been trained in the Western style of riding, and it only belongs in the fingertips of very experienced Western riders. Otherwise it easily becomes an instrument of torture which can quickly and totally ruin the horse.

But what is the real difference between English and Western? In Europe a horse is more or less firmly collected, which means that the reins are held in the rider's two fists as long as it takes for the horse's neck to be raised up and curved, and there is constant contact between the horse's mouth and the rider's hands – in other words a dependency. Influenced by the movement of the rider's buttocks and thighs the horse is thrust forward. Thus the rider is driving from behind and at the same time braking at the front. In the words of sometimes unfamiliar horse jargon the horse is standing on the aids so that it does not collapse.

What must be said at this point is that a reasonable English style rider does not constantly harass his well-trained horse but lets it get on with its work with the least amount of interference, as long as it is doing it correctly. Unfortunately these riders are the exception. Wherever English riding is seen, there are usually one or two riders who are constantly hitting the side of the horse with their heels – which is totally absurd and causes apathy in the horse.

To start with, the same principles apply to Western training: here too the horse is collected so that it learns the correct way to carry the rider's weight and to walk while keeping its balance – meaning with the hind legs clearly moving under the body. Otherwise there is too much pressure on the forelegs and on the back, which can be harmful. When a horse has been fully trained and has learned how to use its legs and its back properly it is ridden with a loose rein and with the rider's fingertips. To a large extent the horse's head and neck are able to move freely about and play their natural role as a balancing pole. Therefore a Western horse is able to balance its weight better, which makes it much more sure of itself in open terrain than most other horses.

To drive and steer a Western horse, a rider uses his thighs and his buttocks and redistributes the weight of his body. For many Western riders voice signals are also very important, and are certainly effective

132 with animals with such excellent hearing; others, however, prefer to ride around in total silence.

It is very important in Western riding that aids – meaning signals using the legs, body weight, reins and voice – are only given when it is necessary. As long as the horse is doing its work as it was taught and as the rider expects, it is left in peace. The horse undoubtedly finds this more pleasant than constantly being dependent on aids. And this is probably a main reason why Western horses, on average, appear noticeably more even-tempered and contented than their European counterparts. Another contributing factor is that, in general, most Western horses are kept under proper conditions.

One other aspect of Western riding should be emphasised here: handling and horsemanship. A cowboy expects his horse to function without any difficulty in any given situation. Its role is to react immediately to the slightest signal and not even to think about resisting. And it is true that Western riders have these very same expectations whether they are participating at shows or quietly cultivating this style for themselves. For example, a good Western horse does not budge from the spot where it is standing when it is being mounted until it receives a signal to do so. This is practiced over and over again until the horse grasps what is expected of it, even if it takes months.

Because it is exposed to all sorts of different unexpected things or frightening sounds while it is being trained, the animal does not scare easily every time it hears a piece of fluttering plastic. After a rider has dismounted it remains standing calmly on the same spot for at least a few minutes, with the reins hanging down to the ground. Not even a pail of oats placed a few steps away from its nose can tempt it.

Even these small examples illustrate that obedience and mutual trust are greatly emphasised in Western riding. And not until you try to teach your horse some of this kind of discipline will you notice what an enormous amount of patience is required. Teaching and training a Western horse is extremely time-consuming. A cowboy calculates that it takes four to six years before he has produced the crack horse that he wants. So you can well imagine that after six weeks of quick orientation a horse will only get as far as the first letter of the alphabet, so to speak.

Naturally performance is also important in Western riding, but priority is given to careful training. Conversely, the main expectation of many European riders is that a horse perform a perfect show jump. There is little evidence of harmonious cooperation between the horse and rider, even among the top riders; some heats are like a duel between the rider and the horse. Banned training methods, which are really forms of animal cruelty, are often applied.

Many European riders can at most spare a sympathetic smile for Western riders – and vice versa. Certainly both methods have their advantages and their justification, and fair riders with horse sense exist everywhere, just as black sheep do.

Among certain people there is the idea that Western riding is easier than the English-style and offers a quicker means of riding out, instead of making the endless rounds on the track. This is a misconception: it is not easier even if it looks more casual and relaxed once it has been mastered. But either way you must learn the proper seating and the right aids. And since most people in Europe only have an opportunity to learn the European riding style (mainly because the nearest Western riding school is located too far away), you should try to ask some questions about training during your riding lesson. Above all, ask your instructor to explain such things to you as: why do we ride in a circle; what is the purpose of "shoulder inwards"; why do we canter out of a circle; why do we always hear "heels down," and so forth? If you know why you are doing something you will understand how to do it more quickly. And if your riding instructor does not have plausible answers to your questions there is something wrong somewhere.

Lunging

For a horse of any age, working on the lunge is an extremely useful extension to working with the rider. It allows the horse to develop a pure gait without the annoying burden of an often poorly seated rider on its back or the rider's aids.

Very few aids are required for lunging, but on the other hand a great deal of concentration and quiet are essential. Simply by using your voice, maintaining good posture and showing complete attentiveness you will succeed in establishing an invisible bond between you and your horse, and produce mutual harmony. Anyone who says that lunging is only good for giving a horse a chance to let off steam before it is taken riding is totally off the mark. You should also avoid allowing a horse simply to run around in a circle, waving a lunge whip about, yelling, letting the lunge drag on the ground or putting it over your head because you are too lazy to turn in the circle yourself.

By using the lunge you can lead your horse around different circles; the lunge

Western riding: it looks easy but is just as difficult as 'English' riding.

Above: The correct way to work a horse outdoors on the lunge.

whip - roughly speaking – replaces your leg action. On the basis of these two aids your charge is exercised. It can move in a relaxed way and swing its back freely. By walking on the circle track the horse's inner side becomes more rounded, whereas the outer neck and rump muscles are stretched. Circling makes the inner hind foot bear more weight and bend lower – an excellent exercise for any horse.

Try it yourself. What you need is a quiet place, preferably a corner somewhere in the riding hall or a fenced in square area. In addition you need a lunge cavesson, a lunge line and a lunge whip. It is preferable not to use a riding bridle because the strap of the lunge in the snaffle rings puts contact on the horse's mouth, and when it is released it can affect the horse's back.

Your voice gives the commands for changing gait, encourages the animal to participate or calms it down when it moves forward too quickly. If your horse has not worked on a lunge before, you will need a helper at the beginning to lead the horse quietly around the circle. First practice changing pace, stopping and quietly standing still, all three of you working together.

Gradually the horse will understand what you are expecting of it and your helper can move away in your direction. Now you take over with your voice and the whip.

If your horse tries to follow your helper, gently raise the whip in the direction of the saddle girth to encourage it to move forward. If the animal still proceeds to step into the inner part of the circle you can usually stop it quickly from doing so simply by extending the whip to the height of its shoulders. If it starts to turn towards you, then you have not been watching out properly. You must be strict and lead it back to the inner circle, let it stand there, walk backwards to the middle of the circle, and again using your voice and raising the whip give the command to move forward. You should always make sure that the horse is stepping out at a good pace but is also relaxed. Using your voice and raising the whip upwards from the ground in the direction of the hindquarters you give your ward the sign that it should either increase its pace or change its gait. By letting the whip drop to the ground or speaking in a deep voice you can command your horse to walk more slowly or to stop.

By slowly pulling in the lunge you can decrease the size of the circle which makes the animal bend its legs even more und use its hindquarters. As you slowly release the lunge the circle track increases to the size you want. You will be surprised at how quickly the horse grasps this fact.

When lunging your horse always remember that these exercises demand that a horse is paying attention, constantly bending its legs and bringing its hindquarters into action. This is hard work. It is advisable to break off the lunging session after half an hour; always lunge in both directions of the circle and be careful to keep your place in the middle of the circle so that the horse does not zigzag. For a change you can also leave the circle once in a while and, with the horse on the lunge, walk straight along the track, do a volte in the corner or even practice swerving and so forth.

There is no need to use side reins on a horse that stretches its head forward and then down during the lunge, unlike a horse which is stiff and steps out with a hollow back. The reins help a horse to loosen up the tension in its neck and back areas.

Every time you change the lunge from one hand to the other or at the end of each lunging session you should leave the horse standing on the circle line and go up to it. In other words, do not pull a horse on the lunge towards you. Otherwise the next time around the horse will no doubt get the idea in the middle of its work to end the exercise itself by running to the centre.

Cavalettis: exercising for relaxation

Every rider's goal is to ride on a horse that is psychologically and physically well-balanced and has stamina. Despite the burden of a rider on its back a horse should be able to keep its balance; its muscles should be relaxed and strong. Cavalettis are excellent aids for this. Cavalettis are large wooden poles which are attached to low cross-struts at both ends. Horses that exercise with cavalettis become very sure-footed because they are required to adjust their movements according to the positioning of the poles. In doing so they are constantly shifting their centre of gravity and learning how to regain their balance quickly. All the important muscles needed for exercising are strengthened, since the horse is lifting its feet higher than usual when walking over the cavalettis. An accurate gauging of the poles demands the animal's full attention and active participation. This exercise offers riders a welcome change and also helps them to get rid of any possible stiffness or tenseness they might have; they too must concentrate, keep their balance as they are going over the cavalettis and relax their hold – the rider forgets to hang onto the horse, pulls on the reins or sits stiffly on the horse's back.

For the walk and trot cavalettis should be placed at a height of 15-20 cm/6-8 in. It is important to make sure that the ground is not slippery; otherwise the horse is apt to tense up. A very good exercise is to let the horse run over the cavalettis on its own – not only because a horse will feel less

Above: Best suited for lunging, the cavesson.

136 tension without a rider on its back and will learn that it need not be afraid of the poles on the ground but also because it gives you a chance to observe its movements. First one cavaletti is placed along a wall or a fence. Pins or bars are used to show the horse the way. If it walks over this single pole without hesitating then gradually three more poles can be added at intervals of 80-100 cm/32-40 in. Now you really must watch carefully: if the horse steps in between the poles, then the cavalettis have been placed too far apart; if it stiffens up and gets into a muddle with the poles, then the intervals are too close together. It takes some patience before a horse is able to walk over the poles willingly and on its own

accord. The sound of your voice and a long lunge whip can help to encourage it.

After the walking phase on both sides of the cavaletti grid it is time for the trot. For this exercise the poles must be 1.3-1.5 m/ 5 ¼-6ft apart from one another. To make the horse understand the exercise a helper can lead it at a trot and then release it right before it reaches the cavalettis. Because this work is very demanding on the horse's muscles and joints, 10 minutes are enough to start. The next step is the work in the saddle, which is done in the same way and in the same sequence as letting the horse proceed on its own. Approach the cavalettis using the driving aids, hold the hands way down and then release the reins just as the horse goes over the bars. You should lean with the top of your body slightly forward and, using your thighs and your knees, shift your weight more to the side of the horse to take the pressure off its back. For the trot the stirrups are fastened somewhat shorter; feel free to use one hand to hold onto the mane to avoid losing your balance. If you feel secure enough, hold your hands down very low and pushed in the direction of the horse's mouth as you go over the poles. The deeper a horse stretches itself forward and downwards, the more it curves its back and strengthens its muscles. If it stiffens up, return to using one cavaletti and ask a helper to observe whether you are sitting properly. Here too it takes some patience before a horse loosens up its back muscles, but you will be rewarded by the marvelous feeling of sitting on a horse which is bright, lively and relaxed in its movements. To avoid the opposite from happening it is advisable to take short breaks, to increase the difficulty of the tasks gradually, to stop after 15-20 minutes and to practice not more than once a week. Try this out with your horse or, during your riding lesson, ask whether the group can do it.

Above: A cavaletti grid is very good for relieving stiffness and tension in a horse and good practice for beginner riders.

Dressage

The word dressage sounds like it means breaking in but – if it is interpreted correctly – it simply refers to the training of a horse. Of course you can simply let yourself be carried about by a friendly horse, experience nature with it and develop a real camaraderie, in short: spend some happy hours in the saddle. This has very little to do with horsemanship. Dressage riders who perform the piaffe (trot-like movements on one spot), the passage or the pirouette show horsemanship at its best. It takes many years of training before a dressage horse can perform these difficult exercises. Perhaps you are thinking that dressage is not for you and you do not want to practice for hours on the riding track, that you would rather just have some pleasant rides out on your pony. But you may also enjoy riding a well-trained horse which does not rebel against you and instead moves in full harmony with you, carries you

Taking a horse through its paces using a cavaletti grid. Horses that are exercised with cavalettis become very sure-footed and also physically well balanced.

gently and comfortably, carries out its work to the best of its natural ability, stays healthy and keeps its mental balance. What is needed to achieve this kind of harmony between horse and rider is a horse which has a pure gait and good balance and is relaxed. And to a large extent this depends on the rider's abilities.

A pure gait is the horse moving forward, its hind legs sufficiently far apart, with an even and springy step, swinging back, neck held high and poll relaxed. So this means no tensed-up back, no draggy hind legs shuffling across the ground, no rigid neck tossed up and no stiff poll. To prevent this you need a soft seat. This is the only way to have steady hands and thighs which gently hug the sides of the horse, and thus the right aids to put the horse at ease and make the ride for you soft and pleasant. Anyone who holds the reins too tightly, uses their thighs to cling to the side of the horse and allows themself to fall into the saddle while trotting should not be surprised if the horse starts to stiffen up and consequently keeps throwing the rider higher in their seat, with the rider then hanging onto the horse even more. A horse that exercises without a rider on its back is usually balanced. The forelegs

mainly serve as support whereas the hind legs carry its body forward. The weight of the rider on the horse's back puts more pressure on an untrained animal's forelegs which, without the necessary action from the rider, can tire out more quickly. Therefore the rider must try to bring his horse in balance again which not only means making the hind legs shift the weight but also moving forwards with the forelegs sufficiently far apart to move some of the weight under its centre of gravity.

Being relaxed is another characteristic of a well-trained horse, or as one experienced riding instructor says: All the energy is used for working and not for resisting. A relaxed horse is physically and mentally well-balanced. Its movements are harmonious, its muscles ripple, its ears stand up and it does not stiffen up or resist the aids of the rider. Trust between the horse and the rider is indispensable for removing the inevitable natural tension which exists before the work out or ride. Even being mounted can cause a horse to become tense or to cramp up. It is therefore important that the rider does not jump roughly into the saddle. As a form of resistance the horse will immediately tense up the muscles in its

Dressage is a sporting event based on elegant movement. **Opposite:** Christine Stückelberger and 'Granat' traversing. **Above left:** In a pirouette to the right. **Above right:** In a passage.

back and maybe even try to bolt. A hard pull on the reins will probably make the horse stop but it will also make it stiffen up even more in the neck and poll area. This reaction will result in considerably more effort for you because it will take you longer to get the horse in a relaxed state again.

If as time goes by you become bored with your riding lessons you should ask yourself what the meaning and purpose is of the exercises. After all they were all developed as the basic training for the horse and the rider. And even if the exercises appear to be a far cry from the artistic dressage movements described earlier, remember: every dressage horse and every dressage rider once started the same way.

Saddles

Of all the different kinds of saddles developed through the centuries there are only two main types which are used today; however these are produced in many different variations.

The English saddle is widely used in Europe as well as internationally in equestrian sports. It originated about four hundred years ago in England as a hunting saddle. The large surface of this entirely new construction of saddle was originally twice the size of what we have today. It was later modified for different types of sports and jumping: dressage, general-purpose saddles or tiny racing saddles are available today. These types of saddles are well suited to the different sports involved. English or European saddles have the added advantage that they are relatively lightweight and affordable in price. The disadvantages are that the surface is rather small, and therefore the weight of the rider is poorly distributed. Often these saddles can cause muscle pains which make the rider cramp up; this in turn causes a horse to baulk or can lead to bruising on the horse. Where bruising occurs, white hair later grows on this area.

Above left: Christine Stückelberger and 'Granat' changing leg at the canter from stride to stride. **Above right:** changing with every second stride. **Opposite:** Success can only be achieved through years of training.

Take a look sometime at how frequently you can see these white saddle bruises, or galls, in the withers area of horses at normal riding stables – and how infrequently these seem to appear on Western horses. Another disadvantage is that because of its rather flat construction it is relatively easy to fly out of this kind of saddle; the correct procedure when riding European style is to use a riding helmet.

In its present form the Western saddle, which is generally becoming more and more popular, originated about two hundred years ago in California. In principle it is a Spanish riding saddle which was modified for the work of the cattlemen – and still looks rather like a monstrosity. This is also reflected in the weight of the saddle: a California saddle for adult riders weighs 12-5 kg/26-33 lb, a similar Texan saddle as much as 15-20 kg/33-44 lb.

Excellent Western saddles are also available, which are made with a synthetic saddletree rather than a wooden one. Consequently these are several pounds lighter. Of course there are smaller and therefore lighter saddles for ponies and for young riders. In any event the extra weight of a Western saddle makes little difference to the horse. The most that can happen is that the rider has a more difficult time saddling the horse.

An important aspect of the Western saddle is that it has a large surface that lies on the horse's back and is much better for weight distribution. It is, therefore, much more comfortable for the horse and the saddle seldom causes any saddle sores. However, even a Western saddle must be adapted to fit an individual horse's back. It really must be tried out on a horse before it is purchased. The withers of Western horses are generally deeper than on European sporting horses. Therefore the main thing to watch for is that the saddle allows enough freedom of movement in the withers area, especially when saddling a European warmblood. A good Western saddle is also comfortable for the rider's buttocks and safer because of the deeper, larger seat.

Some relatively inexpensive Western saddles can be bought: these are mainly mass-produced ones which usually come

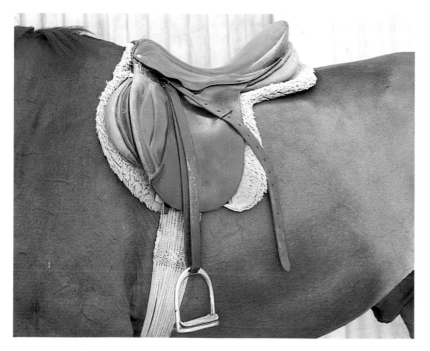

An English saddle modified as a show jumping, dressage, general-purpose or racing saddle is well-suited to the particular type of sport.

from Mexico. These saddles have a limited life. A good Western saddle has always been expensive. A hundred years ago the cost of one of these saddles was equivalent to twenty times more than the price of a horse which had never been broken in, or the yearly wages of a cowboy. But it did last the rider a lifetime.

In principle, a Western saddle is not better than an English saddle, but it is better suited for certain things, such as for riding outdoors, for Western riding and for pleasure and long-distance riding.

Racing: the Sport of Kings

Horseracing has existed since the time when people began to own horses, and over the centuries it has never lost any of its appeal. Very early on, probably even before the ancient Greeks, people tested for speed and endurance in races in order to select the best horses for breeding. Today these types of races still serve as the most important performance tests for breeding. And without a doubt racing is an extremely appropriate sport for horses. What suits the disposition and temperament of a horse more than to race others of its own kind?

There is a significant difference between gallop races and trotting, or harness races. With the latter the horse is usually harnessed to a sulky, a light two-wheeled cart. However the key difference is in the type of gait. In gallop racing the horses run in their natural bounding way. Trotting racing – as the name implies – is done at a trot, a slow gait which is only ever adopted by horses living in the wild when they are changing over from a gallop to a walk, and certainly never when they are in a hurry. Breeding, special training and various mechanical aids – special shoeing, complicated harnessing, and so on – help to ensure that at a trot the horse will reach a racing speed of up to 50 km/30 miles per hour.

A Western saddle is better and more comfortable for the horse and the rider in both recreational and distance riding.

144   **Right:** A touring saddle
developed in France – the rider
sits deep into it, as in a Western
saddle. **Below:** A Brazilian
gaucho. Before mounting his
horse, he places a piece of sheep-
skin over the odd construction
which serves as a saddle.
Below right: An old Turkish
officer's saddle.

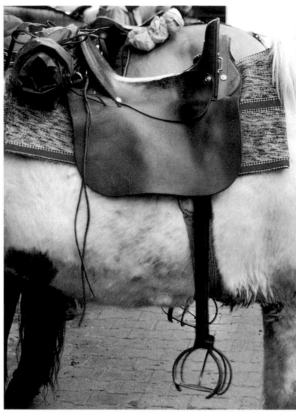

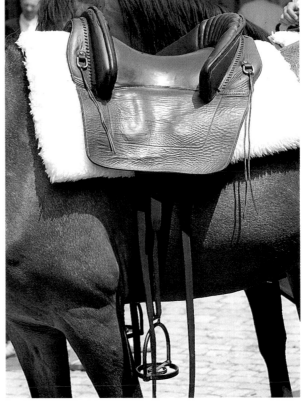

Above left: An Arabian saddle with elaborately decorated and valuable blankets. **Above:** A Portuguese saddle as it is still used today. This is much like the original form of the Western saddle. **Left:** An Arabian saddle with decoration. Note the different shape.

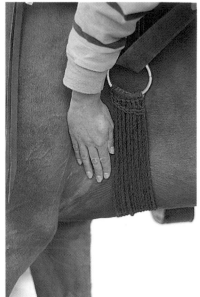

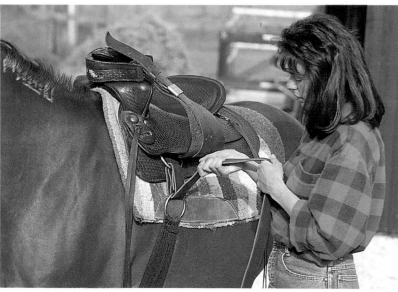

A few tips on the topic of saddles. **Above right:** The long Western saddle girth is looped into a tie knot. **Above:** Whenever saddling a horse, it is important to pull the saddle pad into the gullet of the saddle to prevent putting pressure on the withers. **Left:** During saddling, the girth is initially left fairly loose, and not tightened up until a short time later after the horse has been led or ridden. **Below left:** When the saddle girth is about six inches behind the horse's elbow, then the saddle is positioned correctly.
Opposite: This is the easiest way of bridling any horse.

Here are examples of some of the many bridles available. **Right:** A South American bridle with a curb bit used in riding Paso horses. **Centre:** A Peruvian cavesson. It exerts pressure on the nasal bone and is a gentle bridle particularly suitable for training young horses.

Bottom: A real American hackamore, also bitless, is an excellent bridle for training in Western-style riding.

Above left: A simple curb bit commonly used in Western riding – in the wrong hands a harsh bridle. It should only be used on a well-trained horse and in the hands of a sensitive skilled rider. Used correctly it allows the rider to make subtle movements with the horse. **Above:** The snaffle bridle commonly used in Europe. A basically similar bridle is often used instead of a hackamore in the training of Western-style riding. **Left:** A splendid Arabian bridle – better for showing off than for riding.

On a winning Streak at the Racetrack

The biggest earner among the European racehorses was the German purebred Star Appeal, the galloper of 1975. Another horse of the 1970's, the trotter Bellino II from France, won even more. But the absolute top earner was Spectacular Bid, on a winning streak between 1978 and 1980. More than one hundred years earlier in 1876, Kincsem, a rather non-descript sorrel mare from Hungary very quickly became famous as the Hungarian Wonder. At whatever racetrack she appeared she always left the other horses behind in a trail of dust. Between 1876 and 1879 Kincsem ran a total of 54 races and was never beaten. Only Camarero, which belonged to a Mr. Vidal in Puerto Rico, produced a longer series of wins: from 1953 to 1955 it remained unbeaten in 56 races. After that it ran in another 77 races and was only beaten four times.

When horses race at a gallop they are running in their natural, bounding gait. Horse racing is one of the oldest-known sports.

Even in the heat of a race the horse is not allowed to gallop up repeatedly, is not allowed to continue at a gallop for more than 30 metre/198 ft, or to gallop to improve its position and, finally, not to cross the finishing line at a gallop. Clearly this kind of racing is neither more natural nor more appropriate than, for one example, jumping.

The three-day event originates from the performance tests earlier required of cavalry horses and is therefore also called horse trials. The sight of horses performing military field exercises on television is very impressive, but what is even more splendid is to see this all taking place live on a very difficult obstacle course – it is tremendously exciting to think of having to handle the enormous fences, hedges, embankments, ditches and low jumps with your own horse. There are around 30 moderate to very difficult obstacles on a large cross-country course. They require a great deal of skill from the horse and rider, a high degree of physical preparedness and considerable courage. But this is only the centrepiece of a full three-day event.

The whole event takes three days and begins with a dressage test. The main purpose of this phase is to determine whether the horse has the proper basic training. The hard part comes on the second day: the endurance test. It begins with a ride along a track or road 5 km/3 miles long, which is to be completed at a fast trot of around 15 km/3 miles per hour. This is immediately followed by a steeplechase course of 3500-4000 meter/2200-2500 ft set up with 12 obstacles. This phase is done at a gallop and requires a speed of more than 41 km/25 miles per hour. The average horse would be quite done in after this effort. However, for an eventing horse the finish line of the steeplechase is the starting point of the second stretch which

Above: In harness racing, horses are almost always hitched to a sulky. Whether this is just a sport for horses is something which can be argued.

Right: Steeplechasing. The fences are light and fall over on impact. **Overleaf:** Cross-country. This takes the rider through trenches and over ditches and often very dangerous obstacles.

Jockeys – Featherweights in the Saddle

The Englishman Lester Piggot is probably the most famous jockey in the world, but the American Willie Schoemaker who was born in Texas in 1931 was the most successful one. From 1949 to 1981 he ran in 34,623 races, won more than 8000 of them and made over $8,000,000 in prize money. The great Shoemaker is no more than 150 cm/160 in tall and weighs about 43 kg/95 lbs. An English jockey by the name of Kitchener weighed barely more than just half this much. When he won the Chester Cup on Reed Deer in 1844, he weighed in at just 22.226 kg/48 ½ lb.

Above: How a cartoonist sees obstacles. **Right:** This is how eventers sometimes experience water jumps.

this time is 14 km/9mph again at a trot or gentle gallop. After that there is a 10-minute break during which the vet checks the physical condition of the horses. Only those animals which pass this health test are allowed to the starting line for the last competitive event, the previously mentioned extremely demanding cross-country test.

This means that the rider has now survived the second day but not yet completed the whole event. The third day of competition is the show jumping. Although this is not a particularly difficult test, it shows how well the horses have survived the enormous strains of the previous few days.

In eventing the abilities of the horse and rider are pushed to the limit – and sometimes even exceeded. Today there is a great difference of opinion about this: what many protectors of animals call pure horse slavery is considered by others to be the crowning glory of riding.

Quadrilles

The quadrilles, a complex group riding programme, is totally different from the three-day event but also has military origins. King Philip II of Macedonia, the father of Alexander the Great (the owner of Bukephalos, one of the most famous horses in history), was probably the first person to organise a highly-regimented cavalry. He made his soldiers line up in rows and columns. In formation and with great precision they were required, using different gaits, to ride in a straight line, traverse, ride in a circle, ride towards each other and down through their own rows. The purpose of all these exercises was to train the troops in manoeuvrability and to promote a feeling of order in the

Above and left: Nostaliga. As an interlude, some riding schools practise the old military-style quadrilles.

individual riders as well as to develop agility, willingness and composure in the participating horses.

Exercises of this kind have been part of the training programmes of cavalries everywhere since the time of the ancient Greeks. During the 17th century so-called figure riding was a magnificent display for the aristocracy and in those days had a circus-like air to it. Today quadrilles are sometimes practised at riding schools as interludes for special occasions.

Re-capturing the past in a different style; dressing up the mounted band in historical uniforms.

The horse and carriage through the centuries

The oldest training handbook available on driving originates from about 1350 BC, and was written by a head equerry called Kikkuli who served the Hittite king Suppiluliumas. He recommended that the training of chariot horses begin in the spring and last a period of around seven months. To separate out the good horses from the less suitable ones right at the outset he demanded that during the first few days of training the horses cover long stretches at a pacing gait. As was customary with all chariot horses during ancient times, all of his draught animals were also

fitted with a yoke on their shoulders, which was connected to a harness on their chest. In Kikkuli's opinion, teams were to be kept together for as long as they lived because it took a great deal of training for a horse to become accustomed to a new partner.

In those days chariots were used in battle and for hunting. There was a high regard for the craftmanship that went into building the chariots because of the knowledge and experience required to make a chariot, which was not only as lightweight as possible but also sturdy. For the drivers (who also acted as archers at the same time) it was not easy when going at break-neck speed to keep their balance in a chariot, which was frequently running out of control and bouncing around, to steer the horses and then to succeed in hitting the opponent or the quarry.

But as time went by the people of the ancient civilisations recognised the advantages of riding compared to driving a chariot. Not only as they marched into war but also in battle itself the warriors on horseback were superior to those in the chariots because of their mobility. However, important public figures still continued to drive in chariots as a demonstration of rank. This is how the body of Alexander was brought to Alexandria after his death. His chariot was decorated with gold and precious stones and pulled by no less than 64 horses!

As the horse-drawn carriage lost its military significance it developed more and more into a general means of transport. Teams of horses were already being used by the state postal service in the days of the Roman Empire. The horses were always replaced with fresh animals at the postal stops. Couriers on horseback were used on poor sections of the roads. Carriages for hire were available to normal travellers. It is not difficult to imagine the crush in those days

Top: You do not always need large horses for driving – ponies are just as suitable. **Above:** Even a tiny Shetland pony can be trained to participate in driving competitions.

on the enormous well-developed road network, which was used by the royal postal service and the hired coaches as well as by the aristocracy, the latter with often splendidly decorated and well-fitted carriages.

During the early Middle Ages the breast harness replaced the yoke. Instead of being under a yoke the horses were attached to a harness with a breast plate or a horse collar – similar to that which is used today from which breeching straps led to a trace; this was used to attach each horse individually to the swingle tree. There were no driving seats in those days. The driver rode on one of the animals on the right-hand side in the back and from there drove the other horses.

Country Races

In the rural areas of many countries farm horses, such as the Freiberger horses in Switzerland shown here, are often used for racing. Usually, neither the rider nor the horse is well trained. Some of the races are even run without saddles so the whole event is not totally without its risks. But what is so pleasant about these races is that the most important thing is to have a good time.

Country races with four Freiberger horses harnessed together in a row are just as spectacular as the quadriga races of ancient Rome. They take quite some skill but also a large amount of daring.

During the 15th century, carriages, especially those used for transporting passengers, also underwent further development. The carriage body no longer rested on the axles but was hung with chains or leather straps between support posts, which helped to cushion the impact and made travelling on the bumpy roads much more pleasant.

The 18th and 19th centuries saw tremendous changes in transportation on wheels in the United States and in Europe. More than anything else the stagecoach enjoyed its heydey during the first half of the 19th century. However, it soon had to make way for its main rival, the railway. In England the stagecoach experienced its decline much earlier than in the United States, where it took longer to build the railway lines because of the enormous distances between, for example, the Atlantic and the Pacific coasts. Until well into the 20th century however feeder lines were still being serviced with the help of the horse-drawn vehicles – for passengers as well as for goods.

On the one hand, horse-drawn vehicles have become superfluous in modern times.

A horse-drawn wagon used for everyday journeys in Mexico.

164 On the other hand, the sport of horse-driving is experiencing a renaissance. It has been officially recognised as an equestrian discipline by the International Horse Federation and is enjoying growing popularity. In 1971 the first European four-in-hand driving championship took place. Today most drivers follow the method of managing and holding the reins developed by Baron von Achenbach at the turn of the 20th century. It is at least as difficult to learn how to drive well as it is how to ride.

At the top of the programme in horse-driving is the driver's ability to control his team. Not only is the turnout of the cart, the harnessing and the horses graded but also the presentation of the driver and his helpers. The first test, the dressage, is extremely demanding. The team is required to present the walk and the three types of trot: the collected trot, the extended trot and the working trot. Stopping and standing without moving, moving backwards and performing simple figures such as the serpentine line, the volte and the double volte, show the judges whether the overall impression given by the team, the purity of the gaits, the momentum, the obedience of the horses and the driver's skill in handling the team are worthy of high grades.

On the second day there is the endurance test, during which the judge sits next to the driver in the driving seat. A different pace, such as the walk, the slow trot or the fast trot, is prescribed for each section of the course. Penalty points are given when the driving is too fast or too slow, as the case may be. The driver must be

Horse-driving always requires a great deal of skill and is often combined with elegance.

Horsepower

What is the horsepower of this brewery team?
Six? False. A horsepower is an internationally
recognised technical unit of power. It stands
for the power required to lift up a weight of 75
kg/163 lb a distance of 1 m/39 in in one
second. In reality a horse is 10 to 13 times as
strong.

able to drive through the obstacles at the end of the course; his passengers in the vehicle are allowed to shift their weight in tight turns to help prevent it from tipping over, and to call to the driver as soon as the rear wheels have cleared an obstacle.

The last part of the test is the obstacle driving on the third day. Up to twenty obstacles must be mastered at a speed selected by the driver. Penalty points are given for exceeding the prescribed time limit or knocking over the gates marked by the cones and poles. In this discipline the passengers are required to remain calmly seated – a difficult task.

Long-distance riding and racing

Long-distance riding is a competitive sport. It is a sport that is also tough and can often degenerate into a form of horse cruelty just as almost any other equestrian sport. But when pursued seriously, distance riding is one of the best competitive sports and is also very well suited to the character of horses. However it is not at all an interesting sport for riders who are seeking the applause of the crowds or wanting to earn money. It is a quiet and unobtrusive sport

and needs a great deal of idealism, mainly because of the intensive training required – daily and in all kinds of weather. But no one who has developed a taste for distance riding and has experienced the joy and commitment of the horse in performing its task, will find it easy to give it up again.

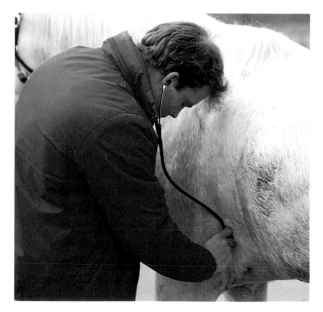

Above and top: Regular examinations by a veterinary surgeon ensure that horses are not over-exerted on long-distance courses. .

There are tests with different levels of difficulty; therefore in principle every rider and every horse with some degree of training can participate. As a beginner you can first try an unranked endurance test, which lets you choose the speed and distance. The minimum distance is 30 km/19 miles, the maximum 160 km/99 miles in one day. A vet examines the horse before you start and then there are regular veterinary checks during the course of the ride. Horses which show signs of over-exertion are removed from the competition.

There is also another kind of long-distance riding test in which the rider must run against the clock. The highest speed is specified at 4, which means a quarter of a mile per minute or 15 km/9 mph. The distance is usually between 30-80 km/19-50 miles. Penalty points are given when the allowed time is exceeded but the rider does not gain anything by completing the course earlier than the set time. So every clever rider tries to use up the time allowed and preserve the strength of his horse as much as possible to ensure that it passes the veterinary checks. Of course these checks occur in this event as well.

In the combined performance test the distance ride is subjected to the same rules as in test run against the clock, but in addition includes an obstacle course, which tests obedience and skill.

Long-distance racing is a serious matter. The victor in this sport is the fastest rider – but in this event no one is allowed to just take off like a maniac on the course. Again the horses are examined regularly for state of fitness, lameness, pressure from the saddle and the girth and so forth. And, as in all disciplines, the rider's interaction with his horse is observed and graded. The minimum distance of a long-distance race is 50 km/31 miles per day, the maximum distance is 160 km/99 miles per day. Only

Achal-Tekkiner

As a rule Arab horses usually take the top places in long-distance racing in Europe and the United States. But there is another breed which is fast becoming a serious competitor to the Arab in long-distances: the Achal-Tekkiner. These extremely noble horses from the open steppes of Turkmenistan and Kazakhastan are a cross between an Arab and an English thoroughbred. For centuries their suitability for breeding has been based on their success in long-distance racing. Here are some incredible figures: Three Achal-Tekkiner stallions covered the distance of 1067 km/663 miles between Chiva in Uzbekistan to the Caspian Sea in seven days – in spite of the fact that they had not had one drop of water for two of those days. In 1988 Turkmen riders on horseback rode 3200 km/1987 miles from their home towns to Moscow and it took them only 60 days. Because of the recent chaos of war in their countries of origin, these extraordinary horses are in great danger. There are a few breeders in western Europe who are trying to maintain the breed with about two dozen breeding animals.

well-trained horses which are in peak form, and highly-experienced riders stand any kind of a chance of winning in these competitions. There is an interesting detail in this connection: as an average, about 80 per cent of all the female participants manage to complete the difficult races compared to only around 55 per cent of the male participants.

Most countries in Europe have associations which organise competitions for long-distance riding . If you are interested in this sport, you can find out everything you need to know from your local association.

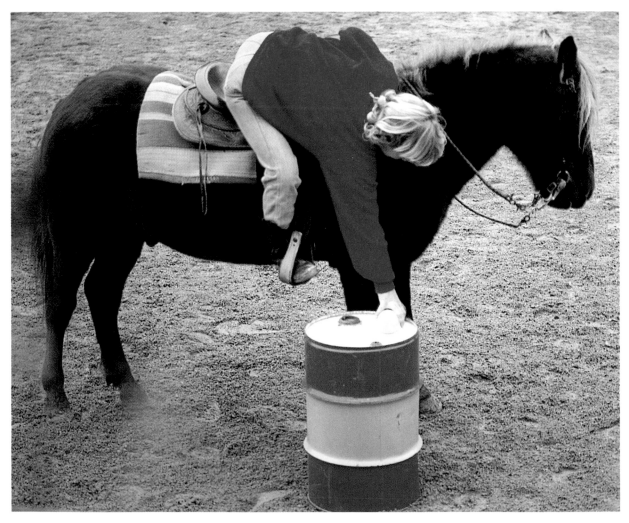

Above, opposite and overleaf: Mounted games are fun and promote skill development and harmony.

Mounted games

Mounted games are as old as riding itself and in some cultures have been preserved until today in their original and mostly rather wild forms – in the endless steppes of Central Asia, in North Africa, in the cattle-raising areas of North and South America as well as in certain other parts of the world. In Europe these games have largely been replaced by more modern forms of horse racing, except for some of the very traditional events such as farm-horse racing in Switzerland, horseshoe-throwing in Austria, ring-throwing in

Polo

Polo was played in Persia more than two thousand years ago. The game was brought to England in the 19th century by English hussar officers who had learned it in India. Today polo is mainly played in England (where Prince Charles is the most famous polo player), in the United States and in Argentina. It is a hard and fast game which demands quick reaction, great skill and good balance from the riders and their horses as well as great harmony between them. Unfortunately polo is also an expensive sport because the cost and maintenance of at least two and preferably three or four horses per player, plus the expense of training and instruction, amount to a great deal of money. There is no financial return: the gain from it is enjoyment and possibly fame and glory.

In polo two teams, each consisting of four riders, try with their sticks to smash a hard white willow ball through the 7.5 metre/25 ft-wide goal post of the opponent. The ponies must be changed between the four to maximum eight playing periods, called 'chukkas', because they are constantly being pushed to the upper limit of their physical ability in this very quick game on a grass field measuring at least 150x250 metres/93x155 ft.

The animals used for riding in the game are traditionally called ponies, but in reality they are light breeds or thoroughbreds with lively temperaments. These horses have the toughness, speed and endurance essential for this team sport.

northern Germany and the very popular gymkhana in Great Britain.

There has been a welcome change from the traditional horse sports during the last few years. More and more horse lovers are gradually becoming tired of monotonous show jumping and the unpleasant practice-training which goes with it for some riders. There are many other more interesting kinds of competitions that can be organised, including obstacle course tests, flag, barrel and slalom racing, touring competitions and tag.

Western riding
as a competitive sport

In Western riding the horse is in a state of natural self-reliance and does not constantly depend on aids, meaning that changes of direction and speed as well as a change of gait are indicated by subtle prompts conveyed through the rider's weight, thighs, hand and voice.

This riding style, which is ideally suited to cowboy work and for riders in open country, requires just as much skill as the European style. And in Western riding as well there are the same masses of mediocre but ambitious riders as well as the equally great exceptions. And often the same things go on here as they do in European riding or in life in general – that those with the real skill do not let their success go to their heads, and seldom can anything be expected of those who take a cocky approach.

Just like anyone else, Western riders also look for ways of measuring their sporting skills. Competitions, which test different skills and are guided by firmly fixed rules, serve this purpose and are held not only in America but also in most Western European countries. They are held for three different classes of competitors: youth, amateur and open.

Competitive trail events are skills tests comprising six different tasks which riders on their horses must perform with maximum ease and composure. Three of the tasks are fixed: to open, pass through and close a gate from the saddle; to walk over four poles lying on the ground; and to walk backwards on a fixed line. Three other tasks - not involving jumps but obstacles - are determined by the competition judge.

WESTERN PLEASURE is a test that evaluates the presentation of the different gaits. All the competitors together form a square. The horses must show how they do the walk, the jog and the lope on both sides while the purity and consistency of the gaits and the obedience of the horse are graded. The jog is a slow trot, the lope a slow gallop. Even while performing these two gaits the horse must give an impression of being at ease and relaxed. In North America the emphasis on the horse being relaxed has been carried to such an extreme that its nose almost hangs to the ground and it looks like it is about to fall asleep.

REINING involves a good deal of action. It makes both rider and spectators aware of the kind of temperament hidden in the normally very relaxed Western horse. This gallop test calls for sliding stops (stopping immediately by sliding on the hind legs), spins (quickly turning around with the hind legs standing still), rollbacks (fast half-turn on the hind legs and then set off in an immediate gallop) and quick walking backwards. The riders are also graded on the basis of precision of movement while galloping at clearly different speeds on the designated lines and circles.

WESTERN RIDING is a dressage test on designated lines and circles – in their entirety these figures are called patterns – consisting of opening and closing a gate, stepping over a pole and eight sliding stops at fixed locations. The grading is based on fluid and accurate presentation.

SUPERHORSE is a demanding test; it is a combination of trail, pleasure, and Western riding and reining. It shows the capabilities of a good all-rounder. The competition only applies to the open class.

SHOWMANSHIP at the halter involves riding and leading the horse by hand to the judge.

Previous page: Barrel racing involves negotiating three barrels set up in a triangle on a cloverleaf-shaped course.
Left and opposite: Skill is paramount in trail riding. A horse trained for this Western discipline will have the right skills for riding in open country.

The horse is to let itself be led willingly and stand quietly and correctly during the judging. This test, for the amateur and youth classes, emphasises correct turnout in the rider and in the horse.

HALTER is a test that evaluates the horse's physical appearance; it is particularly important in the breeding of Quarter horses. The horse is graded on the basis of its conformation which should comply with the correct characteristics of its breed and on the quality and harmony of its movements.

Above: Competitions in Western riding require skilful and talented riders who are able to direct their horse over difficult courses.

HEALTH AND AILMENTS

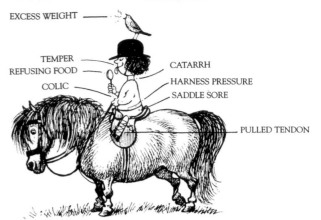

EXCESS WEIGHT

TEMPER
REFUSING FOOD
COLIC

CATARRH
HARNESS PRESSURE
SADDLE SORE

PULLED TENDON

No doubt every good rider and horse owner would prefer a horse which is in top condition. Therefore regular health checks are important to ensure that any ailments are detected at an early stage and that the work being demanded of a horse is not beyond its capabilities. How do you go about this? Take the time every so often to observe the behaviour of your horse or pony, and ask yourself the following questions: is the animal unusually agitated or suddenly listless; is it eating less; and is it oblivious to its environment? Is its posture strange; is it constantly standing still; are its limbs stiff; are there long periods when it will not stand up, or days when it does not lie down? Conspicuous or odd behaviour should always be taken seriously.

Next, take a close look at the horse's coat: does it lie flat, and is it smooth and shiny? Note, however, that not all horses have naturally silky-smooth coats, especially those horses that are kept at grass. These horses can sometimes look shaggy, particularly in winter when their hair is long.

A sweating horse that has not undergone any physical exertion, and loss of hair in a particular place, may both be signs of poor health. If the animal also tends to rub these bald spots at every opportunity, then parasites may be the problem. Healthy skin is elastic. You can easily test this yourself by taking between your fingers a fold of skin from the neck of your horse or pony and lifting it gently. When you let it go, the fold should disappear immediately.

As with people, ailments in horses are frequently accompanied by fever. The normal body temperature of a horse is between 37.5° and 38.4° Centigrade. You take the horse's temperature by inserting a thermometer in its rectum, but if you have never done this before you should leave this to your vet. Other ways of checking the health of your horse include looking at the colour of the conjunctiva of the eye, and of the mucous membranes of the nostrils and the mouth. Both should be a bluish-pink. To check the conjunctiva, gently open the horse's eye with your thumb and index finger. Aside from a deep redness caused by over-exertion, every other colour deviation is a sign of illness.

You can check your horse's pulse on the lower edge of its lower jaw, in the indentation in front of the masseteric muscle (the muscle that moves the lower jaw); or on the left side of the chest wall behind the elbow bumps. You should be able to determine a minimum of 28 and a maximum of 40 beats a minute. In ailments accompanied by fever the pulse rate is high, as it is naturally with strenuous exertion. Well-trained horses recover very quickly from hard work, and their pulse rates soon return to normal levels. As a preventive measure, horses with pulse rates which are too high in spite of short rest periods, are apt to be disqualified during long-distance riding or eventing.

If you position yourself at an angle behind the horse, you can monitor its respiration by the movement of its flanks. Ten to fourteen breaths per minute are normal. Coughing and irregular breathing or a dripping nose are signs of a problem affecting the respiratory organs.

What is most important for the well-being of a horse is its eating and drinking

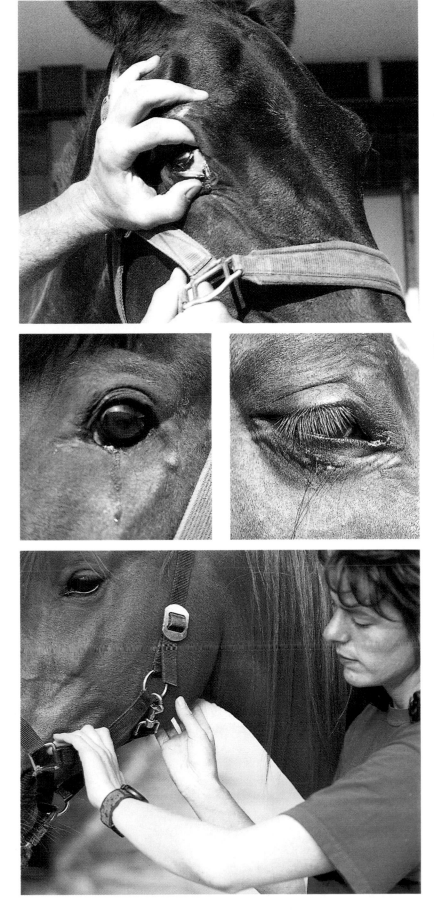

Left: This is how to examine the conjunctiva inside the eyelid. An expert is able to determine signs of illness based on colour deviation. A healthy horse has clear eyes.

Centre: Dull eyes (left) or inflamed eye rims (right) are disorders which must be taken seriously. This is something for the vet to attend to.

Left and above: Using the tips of the fingers, the horse's pulse can be felt on the inner surface of the lower jaw, or in the cavity on the side of its leg .

habits, regular excretion and the colour and hardness of its stool. Anything which is not the norm – lack of enthusiasm during feeding, lack of interest in touching anything, failure to excrete or pass urine for long periods of time, indications of being in pain when passing water – should be viewed as an alarm signal. Before you ring the vet, you should always check to make sure that there is nothing wrong with the horse's feed or water.

Now to the actual ailments. A general knowledge of the most frequent symptoms of illness in a horse can be of help to you. This will enable you to take preventive measures and ensure that you do not ignore any of the first warning signs, or get into a panic. Remember: it is better to ring the vet too often rather than too infrequently.

WORMS

A wide variety of worms can attack a horse: threadworms, roundworms, lungworms and tapeworms, stomach botts and so forth. But horses have learned to live with worms; in fact a horse will seldom be totally free of them. It can manage very well with a small infestation, but the conditions under which horses are now kept, particularly the fact that they are kept in restricted spaces, increase the risk of massive worm infestations, which can be life-threatening. By examining a horse's stool laboratory technicians determine the type of worm with which it is plagued. This ensures that the appropriate treatment will be provided.

Worming should always be carried out in the spring before the horses are turned out to graze, otherwise the whole field can become infested with worms. It has also proved worthwhile to allow horses to graze on an alternating field basis, or from section to section. Horses in open stables must be dewormed more frequently than those in boxes. One way to try to prevent worms is by keeping the stables clean, frequently changing the straw, picking up the manure in the paddocks and the fields, and stacking the dung. The heat emitted from the inside of a dung heap kills certain worm eggs. In spite of this, fields where horses are put out to graze should not be fertilised with material from the stable.

TICKS, FLIES AND HORSEFLIES

The bite of a tick can often cause severe itchiness to a horse. Ticks are bloodsuckers which also can carry disease. After riding through damp woods or along a row of hedges you should examine your horse for ticks and, if necessary, use alcohol to remove and destroy them. Do not forget about yourself in the process ticks can also attach themselves to humans. Flies are annoying pests and the temperament of a horse affects the degree of its defensive reaction to them. Sensitive horses can be fitted with ear protection combined with a "fly whisk" made of fabric or strips of leather attached to the browband. Clean stables and the regular removal and proper stacking of the dung also help. The heat within the dung heap destroys fly incubation. A variety of preparations are available on the market for warding off horseflies and other insects. Unfortunately they are only effective for a limited period of time, have an unpleasant smell and can irritate the skin.

ECZEMA AND RINGWORM

Eczema is an infection of the outer layer of skin. The hair on the affected areas becomes dull and coarse and falls out. You can see tiny lumps, scurf or scabs on the skin. It appears most frequently in the saddle area where the sweat is not able to evaporate properly. Eczema on the tail combined with the horse's urge to relieve the itching by scratching against something

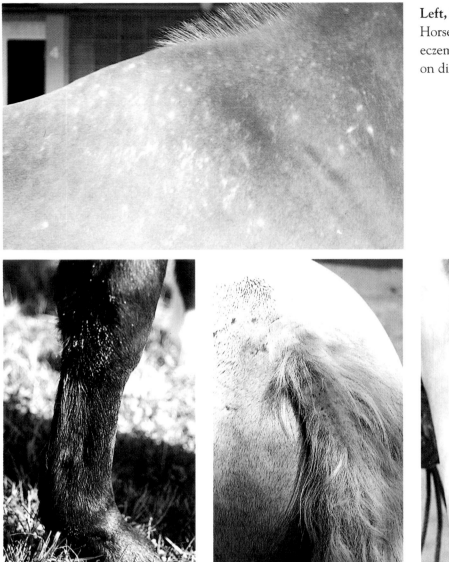

Left, below left and centre: Horses can be afflicted with eczema or fungal skin infections on different parts of their bodies.

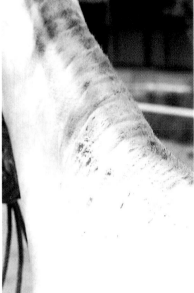

Above: Flies lay their sticky eggs in the hair on a horse's legs, and these eggs can develop into dangerous intestinal parasites if the horse rubs them off with its mouth. The treatment depends on the instructions given by the vet – the sooner the better.

is a sign of worm infestation. Eczema on the pasterns is called malanders which causes redness of the skin. The fluid which is secreted combined with dirt forms a grimy layer or scab. Treat it by cleaning it with a dry clean cloth and then applying a mild ointment. You must never shave the hair from that spot; otherwise the hair bristles dig into the sensitive skin with every movement the horse makes.

Ringworm can enter through the surface of the skin from small sores. It is recognisable by small round or oval patches where the hair has broken off. It mostly appears

First-Aid Kit for the Stable

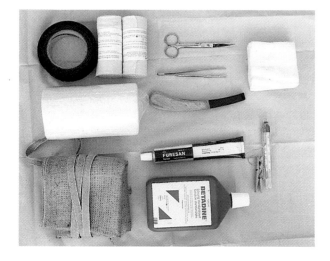

Every reputable stable should be equipped with a first-aid kit that is regularly checked to ensure that all the medicines and materials are in good order and have not exceeded their expiry dates. As a matter of course when checking the contents you should throw away anything that is old and cannot be identified.

Drugs and materials that are usable should be put with their original packaging and placed in a special box, together with the telephone numbers of the veterinary surgeon and his locum. It is also very helpful to attach an inoculation and deworming schedule. In an emergency, the vet will be able to tell at a glance when the animal was last inoculated or dewormed.

Horses should be inoculated regularly against contagious viral coughs, tetanus and, depending on the area, rabies. Thanks to the list there will be no gaps in the worming scheduled when the date for worming falls due. If the vet comes along to give an inoculation, he can be asked to check the horse's teeth at the same time. With the horse's one-sided chewing action small bumps can form on the molars, which will make chewing more difficult or even cause bleeding to the mucous membranes inside of the cheek. The following items have proven to be very useful in first-aid kits for stables: iodine tincture for disinfecting around injured areas; a preparation for cleaning small superficial injuries; a medicated ointment containing, for example, cod-liver oil and zinc; gauze bandaging; elastic bandaging; cotton wool in a roll; sticking plaster to be used as dressing material; special cotton wool for stopping bleeding; an ointment containing camphor which stimulates the circulation and has a warming effect; a cooling ointment to relieve bruising caused by saddle or girth pressure, and to apply to limb compresses to alleviate strained tendons; a worming preparation; bayleaf oil for massaging the area around the coronet; and, last but not least, a clean pair of scissors. Ask the vet for help: he or she will no doubt gladly help you set up a simple first-aid kit for the stable.

around the saddle or girth area where the skin becomes irritated. Therefore make sure your horse avoids contact with infected horses; keep grooming materials, drinking pails and other stable supplies clean and do not allow them to be shared by other horses. A good balanced diet is the best protection for a horse. Vitamin and mineral deficiencies and unbalanced diets high in protein and fat promote these afflictions. Regular worming is also appropriate in recurring infestations. Special worm-treatment solutions are something which should be left up to the vet.

WOUNDS

You can treat abrasions to the skin, small cuts and superficial wounds, but open and heavily-bleeding wounds should be handled by the veterinary surgeon. While waiting for the vet to arrive you should cover the wound with a clean cloth to try to stop the bleeding and apply a pressure bandage. Do not change this bandage because the disintegrating blood corpuscles promote the clotting of the blood and stop the bleeding.

To prevent your horse wounding itself you should search the stable and the fields regularly for pieces and bits of plastic and other dangerous materials.

BRUISES AND CONTUSIONS

Poorly-fitting saddles and harnesses can cause swelling, redness or extreme tenderness. Always use a saddle that fits properly, with a large enough surface, no broken saddle trees and a saddlecloth which absorbs the sweat effectively; only ride with a clean bridle with no hooks or bits of iron sticking up. When saddling, place the blanket on the horse so there are no folds in it. The saddlecloth under the saddle should not press against the withers. It is better to leave the girth loose at first, tighten it after a few steps and then sit up properly. Examine your horse's back in the girth area

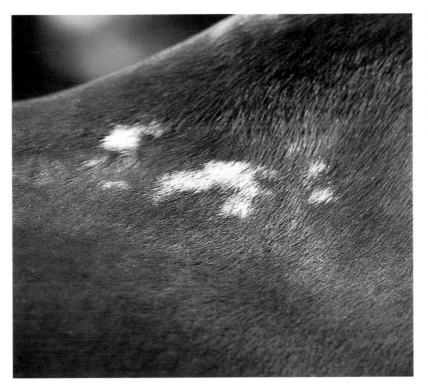

Left: Poorly fitting harnesses and saddles can cause bruising. Saddle sores or galls are fairly common; they can be recognised because of the growth of white patches of hair. The main cause is the small seats of English saddles.

182

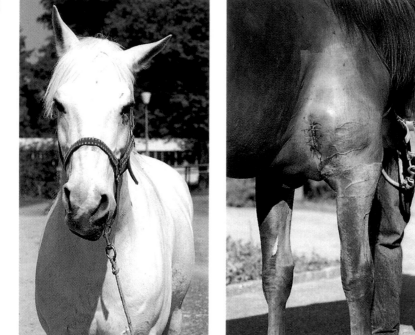

Far left: The position of the left ear is an indication of a tumour in the ear, which has caused paralysis in half of this horse's face. **Left:** A scar resulting from an operation to remove a glandular abscess.

after unsaddling. You should react immediately and call the veterinary surgeon if you see any painful swelling.

RESPIRATORY AILMENTS

Breathing in fumes, vapours and dust can cause inflammation of the mucous membranes of the nose. More frequently however germs or a virus are the reason for respiratory ailments. With a mild form of inflammation a watery or mucous type of substance is discharged from the nose and the horse sneezes and puffs. A simple cold will usually cure itself. It becomes a different matter when the discharge from the nose is yellow mucous and the horse has a fever and shows signs of listlessness. If the horse is not treated immediately by a vet the virus can start to affect the frontal sinuses, the windpipes and even the lungs. Warm and musty stables, dusty hay and too frequent sweeping of the stable gangway encourage the outbreak of these types of ailments.

PROBLEMS WITH THE DIGESTIVE TRACT

Everyone who owns a horse has a fear of colic. This is not the name of an actual illness but refers to the symptom, which is stomach pain. Colic can develop as a result of many types of stomach and intestinal disorders, including constipation and flatulence. It can also occur if there are any problems affecting the urinary track or the sexual organs, or with infections. Horses with mild colic paw the ground, repeatedly lie down at odd times, rise up again and and drop their head down to their stomach. In a severe attack the horse may actually throw itself on the ground and roll around, while sweating heavily. If so, take the horse for a walk until the vet arrives. A sudden drop in body temperature – perhaps as a result of drinking ice cold water, a change in the weather or diet and spoiled feed – can cause colic. Horses which are looked after properly, exercised, dewormed regularly, fed well and allowed enough time to eat and digest their food seldom develop stomach aches.

AZOTURIA

This illness is caused by the accumulation of a high-protein carbohydrate, glycogen, in the croup, loin and upper thigh muscles. The glycogen is broken down too quickly, producing surplus lactic acid that destroys part of the muscle fibre. The symptoms include sweating, trembling and stiffness in the hinds limbs. You can even feel the joints in the hind legs buckling.

The cause of the trouble is sudden strenuous exercise following a period of inactivity in the stable when the horse was fed a monotonous diet. As soon as the symptoms appear return the horse immediately to the stable and call the veterinary surgeon. While you are waiting for the vet to arrive rub the stiff muscles with a heat-producing preparation and wrap the limbs in bandages.

Below: Horses are often very valuable animals. Consequently it pays to invest in good treatment. Medicine practiced on horses today is of a high standard.

If there is no one who can exercise your horse while you are away and turn it out to graze, then you should ensure that your horse is given a reduced amount of high-protein feed during your absence. These measures should then prevent the occurrence of azoturia.

LAMINITIS

Unfortunately this inflammation appears frequently in ponies and in most cases is caused by incorrect feeding and care. If your pony suddenly develops stiffness in the pastern, coffin, and pedal bones, and is walking on the back part of the hoof, if the hoof wall is warmer than usual and your animal winces with pain when you press on it or tap it, it could be suffering from laminitis and needs to be treated.

Laminitis, or founder, is an inflammation of the hoof which can become chronic and very dangerous. Surplus histamine, a substance which breaks down albumin and is contained in feed such as fresh grains and grass, increases the porosity of the vessels in the horny wall of the hoof, causing it to bleed. This causes the laminae to separate from the wall of the hoof, thus loosening the connection between the pedal bone and the hoof capsule. Consequently the tip of the pedal bone drops and presses against the sole of the hoof. This is accompanied by a painful swelling of the laminae.

The process is a complicated one which, unfortunately, can cause the pedal bone to collapse within just three days. The sooner the disease is treated, the better are the chances of success. Sadly, founder is often a tragic cause of death in ponies.

Left: Hooves must be looked after, trimmed and usually also shoed regularly. Even donkeys' hooves require care.
Right: This donkey shows many signs of illness caused by lack of care. It should really be taken away from its owner .

Stress and fear, in the horse as well as in the rider, disobedience, bad habits and mistakes made in the heat of the moment can often be observed in riding schools, with people riding out on their own and at competitive events. One attempt to avoid this is to become stricter and use tougher aids, combined with an approach aimed at showing an animal who is in charge, with the result that riding these horses becomes even less satisfying and more problematic.

Fortunately an American, Linda Tellington-Jones, took an interest in discovering the real causes of this type of behaviour and, along with her partner Ursula Braun, developed a type of therapy for difficult horses. Their work, specifically with problem animals, led to some surprising revelations: the primary reason why problems occur is that most horses lack proper training and their riders and owners do not know the best way to convey their wishes and intentions. The two women also recognised that much of the bad behaviour and obstinacy in horses is caused by physical deficiencies, in other words to ailments affecting the bone, muscle and tendon apparatus which create pain and tenseness. The remedies they use for therapy are simple: good powers of observation, proper use of the hands, a crop, a halter, a lead rein and some ground poles. However, the prerequisite for success in training horses is an abundance of time and a willingness to be patient enough to develop a proper understanding with them.

As a first step the horse therapists recommend that you take a good look at the problem horse, study its conformation and with a gentle touch of your fingers probe all the different parts of its body. Many horses react to the pressure of a person's fingers on different areas by jumping up, pulling away, buckling their legs or tensing up the respective muscles. They use body language to show where they have pain or where something is not right. They could have swelling in the saddle area, a small sore in their coats or stiff muscles.

Odd behaviour, such as refusing to budge, bolting, hitting something with their head or displaying signs of nervousness, is often an expression of pain in a particular part of the body. Even a lay person should be able to find out what is wrong, and with an awareness of which situations are provoking the odd behaviour one can set about eliminating the causes. Is it a saddle with too small a seat, a martingale strapped too tightly or poorly-fitted harnessing which is causing the horse to thrust its head and neck upwards in pain

Right: Two people at the same time practising the 'Tellington touch', a special way of using the hands to feel a horse's body for possible disorders.

thereby pulling away from the reins or perhaps blocking the movement of its hindquarters? Even trying out a different type of saddle or harness could produce positive results.

An alternative is to extend the therapy and retrain the horse from scratch. This should be carried out by working with obstacles such as the 'star', which improve the horse's footing. It also promotes its ability to learn, relieves stress, improves limb co-ordination and develops the horse's sense of balance.

Right: In the so-called 'star' the horse is required to look ahead carefully and judge the distance before lifting each foot and placing it far enough forward so that it ends up standing securely on all fours, between the movable poles, without causing any of them to roll.

Centre: Exercises in which the horse slowly steps sideways and walks backwards promote balance and limb coordination.

Bottom: When it is driven from the ground the horse becomes accustomed to contact with a rope and this later helps to prevent a tendency in it to take flight when it is under a rider or instance, when coming into contact with electric fencing in the pasture. At a later stage of the exercise the horse also learns how to stop, turn, walk backwards and patiently wait for other signals – again without someone leading it by its head.

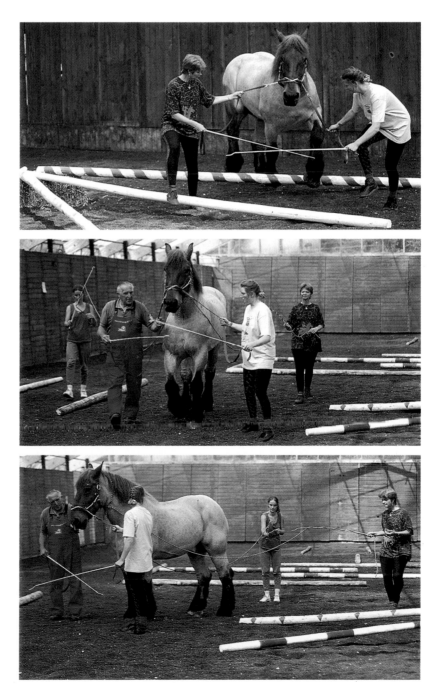

Riding is far less about courage than about skill, consideration, good manners and safety. Of course there is always a risk associated with riding, because in the end it involves two totally different beings who do not always share the same opinion. But it is possible to keep this risk to a minimum and to learn how to handle your horse sensibly in every situation.

Riding on an indoor riding track.

In the indoor hall certain rules are to be observed to avoid any kind of confusion during instruction or while the indoor hall is open for general use. Even before riding into the indoor riding hall every rider should ask in a loud voice from the other side of the closed doors whether it is permissible to enter. You should never enter the hall on your horse until you have received an answer in the affirmative. Once you have entered, then ride immediately to the centre area to minimise any disruption to the other riders.

A group receiving instruction has priority over a single rider. So when a group is riding directly on the edge it has priority. Riders who are practising on their own are required to move to the centre of the hall. In general, priority is given to riders who are riding on the left-hand side (that is, counter-clockwise), trotting, galloping or are making use of the entire track. Those who are riding on the right-hand side (that is, clockwise), stopping or practising voltes and turns are required to make way for these riders. If everyone is riding in the same direction and one of the riders suddenly wants to overtake the others at a faster gait, then that rider moves to the inside and is careful to avoid getting too

close to any of the other riders or cutting anyone off when moving back in again. An indoor riding hall is a place for learning how to ride and for practising, therefore you should go about your activities quietly and not disturb the concentration of the others.

Riding outdoors

Every beginner's dream is to be able to ride outdoors the first time they are on the horse. Anyone who feels secure on a horse after riding for many hours on an indoor riding track but is still afraid of riding outdoors should be able to say so without being laughed at by the others. Fear as a constant companion is an obstacle in riding, yet extreme caution is advisable. There are many things which can distract both the horse and the rider: wind murmuring in the trees, dogs barking, motor noise from cars and tractors, cowbells jingling, pedestrian footsteps, plastic bags flapping on the ground, a child screaming in a car and so forth. It is no wonder that horses are initially afraid of riding along roads and over fields. But if they are given enough time and opportunity to familiarise themselves with everything new around them they will quickly learn to keep calm in almost any situation.

With a very nervous horse the solution may be to take the horse for a long walk and let him sniff and smell everything that is new to him. This will give you a chance to become familiar with the sections of the route which frightened him and find out how you can calm him down and instil confidence in him. You will no doubt find that each time you go out riding, at first in the company of a quiet fellow rider and then on your own, you will continue to become less and less afraid. There is no shame in feeling afraid. It is always better to dismount and take a close look around rather than to clench one's teeth and tense up all over thereby giving the horse the message that danger is around the corner.

In any event you must dismount when you come to an underpass or a narrow bridge, and when going over steep, slippery paths. When riding uphill take the pressure off the hind legs of the horse by gently leaning forward, loosening the hold on the reins and, if necessary, grabbing the horse's mane or putting your hand around its neck. When riding downhill do not lean backwards – a common mistake – but rather sit firmly upright in the saddle or slightly lean forward.

You should always approach sloping areas straight on and not from the side; otherwise there is a danger of slipping. Outdoors you can usually ride an easy seat, but this does not mean standing in the stirrups and being glad about not feeling the unpleasant bumps when trotting. When riding, the rider's seat must never lose contact with the saddle because in a sudden stop you should be able to sit back into the seat and gently move with the motion of the horse and not against it.

There are many things you learn in an indoor riding hall which you can apply outdoors: alternating left and right canter, altering your weight on an extended light trot, rising on an opposite diagonal. You can also ride a small slalom between the trees in the woods (but only if the ground is free of vegetation), using small obstacles such as cavalettis.

You should only ride out alone if you feel totally secure about it. Your horse will notice. Try to change gaits so your horse does not simply imitate the animals in front

A helmet is not only for use on a motorbike – it is jusr as important when riding horses.

of it. If you are riding in a group, the calmest horse should be the one at the front with the more temperamental ones behind it; timid animals should ride in the middle of the group. Again a horse with a quiet nature should form the rear. It is impolite to overtake for no obvious reason or without warning and can also be dangerous if the animals start kicking. Horses have a pecking order which you should also observe when you are riding; so keep your distance from the other horses and never race.

Consideration should always be given to the least experienced riders in a group. They should not be abandoned if their horses happen to refuse to take a certain path or prefer not to gallop. It is also difficult for experienced riders to ride away from a group with their horse or continue at a walking gait if other riders are racing around. Riders at the front should always make sure that the others are behind them. It is dangerous to change pace without advance notice and not to wait until all the others are ready, especially if the riders at the front simply trot or gallop off when turning off into suitable terrain while the riders at the back are still at a walking gait on an asphalt road, or they cannot see the others through the trees, hedges or other obstacles. The sound or sight of other kindred spirits bounding off is the one thing more than anything else that encourages horses to copy unruly behaviour.

There should be enough concern for a horse's health that it is only galloped on dry and safe terrain. Respect for the property and the work of farmers and forest wardens will also ensure that fewer signs prohibiting riding are put up. In principle, considerate riders never take their horses through freshly planted fields, fields of hay or sections of newly planted trees in the forest. Riders should rein in at a walk when they see wild animals and continue to ride like this so as not to disturb them. The animals living wild in our forests are less frequently likely to flee from the sight of horses than from hikers but they suffer enough stress as it is from the large numbers of people seeking relaxation in their living space.

Fighting monotony

It is safer for you and for your partner if you add some variety to your routine when working with your horse and riding it. If a horse starts showing signs of boredom and weariness, it will also soon lose its vitality and interest in performing. Every lesson you demand, whether it is in dressage or in jumping, would then have to be carried out with resistance from the horse. This is not wise, and is dangerous as well: the horse

Signs prohibiting riding should be observed – there is usually a good reason for the the prohibition.

will tense up its muscles instead of relaxing them, jump to the side just before it approaches a hurdle or abruptly refuse to make the jump. The work should be a joy for all the participants involved; it is preferable to cut short a practice session if a horse shows that it has had enough. If you are not having any success with a difficult exercise, it is recommended that you try something easier instead and then praise the horse generously for its efforts. Things will then be better next time around.

Always ask yourself what you have achieved each day. Have you communicated well with your horse? Was the horse content when it returned to its stall? All you need is a little bit of fantasy to put some variety into your routine and thus liven up your riding programme. For example, do not always take the same paths when riding outdoors or start to trot or gallop at the exact same places. Horses remember these things very quickly and then next time will not wait for your aids before storming ahead. If on the other hand they are uncertain about what is going to be asked of them next, they become much more attentive: they do not stumble as soon as the ground becomes a little uneven, shuffle about lethargically or only come alive again when they notice that they are returning to the stable.

There is so much for you and your horse to do together: walking, riding a free rein on the indoor track or on the riding ground, lunging, working with a lead rein and leading it by the hand. If you are ill or on holiday, someone else can exercise your horse for you without the weight of a rider on its back but still in the company of other horses show it a good time.

Working all the time is monotonous, and taking a break is also good for the horse. But, on the contrary, standing in a stall is not relaxing for a horse. The best way for it to relax and to recover its

strength after a session of work is for you to let it run freely in a field, if possible together with other horses, take a long ride at a walking gait with a long rein outdoors, do some light climbing or even a gentle gallop which allows it to get rid of the tense feeling left over from its work.

Transport

Anyone who is fortunate enough to have a horse trailer and is regularly able to explore new scenery or to participate at tournaments and horse shows should also think about the safety of their horse.

Horses should be covered when they are being transported because there is always a draught from the open back of the trailer. Special travelling boots will reduce the danger of injury to the legs, the coronets or the balls of the feet of nervous horses and

Horses Worth Millions

At an auction of thoroughbred yearlings on 20 July 1981 in Kentucky, Robert Sangster threw down 3.5 million dollars for a one-year old horse. The yearling did not have much to offer on its own, except for a very famous father, Northern Dancer. But the most expensive horse is, and remains, Easy Jet – born in 1967 and the 1969 winner of All American Futurity. It was acquired by a syndicate in October 1980 for thirty million dollars. This amount of money could have been used to buy about six thousand ponies at an average price of seven thousand Swiss francs.

during sudden breaking manoeuvres. Saddles and harnessing equipment should be removed before departure; a sturdy stall halter is advisable. The horses should be loaded onto the trailer quietly to avoid any unnecessary excitement to them before the journey starts. A trip in a trailer is strenuous for the horses: they must balance their entire bodies whenever the vehicle is making a turn, accelerating or breaking.

At the end of a particularly quiet peaceful trip the horses should be gently awakened; after they have been unloaded they should be given a chance to accustom themselves to their new surroundings. So before you ride off you should perhaps first brush your horse, lead it around by its halter or ride it at a walk. The more pleasant the horse's experiences are during loading and transport, the more willing and accommodating it will be the next time you want to take it on a journey.

Traffic rules

As a general principle you should ride at a walking gait on the right side of the road when in traffic. This also applies when you are walking your horse on a lead rein. Riders in a group ride one behind the other at a safe distance of one body length between them. When crossing the road all the riders should follow the sign of the top rider and cross together, at the same time preserving the required minimum distance between them. When crossing a road as a group you must also ensure that a gap in traffic is big enough to allow all the riders time enough to cross safely. The distance between the individual horses should not be so big that drivers of cars or of other vehicles feel they can drive through the group. Horses which are forced to stop and are left behind can easily become fidgety. Riders must be particularly careful when on or near roads during dusk or at night. It is compulsory in some countries for a horse to wear reflective boots on all four legs and for the rider to have a light which shines white towards the front and red towards the back attached either to the boot or arm.

Taking responsibility

As a matter of course, every rider should take out accident and third-person public liability insurance.

Anyone who signs up for riding lessons, hires a horse for riding or is even only exercising a pony of a best friend away on holiday, is wise to enquire beforehand who is resposible for damages in the event of an accident and that you and the horse are adequately insured. Every responsible horse owner will take out insurance cover which, at a minimum, should cover them against claims from third parties and for damages arising out of accidents caused by the horse. In many instances the insurance will also cover vet fees should the horse be injured or become ill. But will the Horse Owner's policy also protect you ? If you injured the horse while riding would the owner or their insurance company expect you to pay – irrespective of any insurance cover which is in force?

Public liability cover protects the horse owner from claims made against them by third parties for injury or damage to their property. Just imagine, your horse runs into a pedestrian or makes a car driver swerve thus causing a cyclist on the other side of the road to fall and break their leg. As the rider and therefore the person in charge of the horse at the time, you are basically responsible. You should therefore make sure

the owner's insurance also allows you to ride the horse for the specific purpose for which you intend to use the horse.

Of course, you may also be injured in an accident, and in such a case the horse owner's policy is unlikely to cover your injuries. You should therefore make sure that you have adequate accident insurance to cover you.

Therefore, in much the same way as you would not drive a car before checking the insurance, before you ride a horse, check that you have the horse adequately covered.

And do not forget: clever heads are protected with a wellfitting riding helmet.

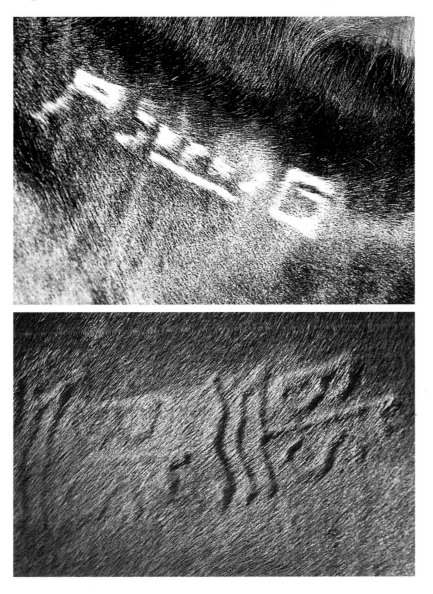

Horses can be differentiated from one another based on a large number of identifiable features; very seldom do two horses look exactly the same. Yet many horses are marked. Arabs, for instance, are freeze-branded with a freeze marker which has been chilled beforehand. White hair grows back on the area which was branded, and is similar in appearance to the scars caused by saddle bruising. **Left:** The brand represents a code which is also entered in the horse's registration papers. **Bottom:** A hot iron is used to brand the stable or stud mark on the skin. With racehorses identification numbers are usually tattooed on the inside of the lips.

NOTES

NOTES

NOTES

NOTES

Achal-Tekkiner 20, 167
Adonis eye 102
Amazons 45
Anatomy 6
Andalucian 83
Appaloosa 80-1, 87
Arab horses 72-3, 76-7
    English breeding, in 71, 74-76, 78
    first progenitor 74
    origins 70-1
    trading in 71
Arabian bridle 149
Arabian saddle 145
Arabs, the 38
Ardennais, French 81
Assyrian horse groomers 32
Attila 37
Azoturia 183

Barrel racing 173
Bashkir Curly 82
Beech, common 103
Belgian 78
Bellino II 150
Box tree 103
Bracken 102
Branding 195
Brazilian gaucho 144
Breaking in and training 36-7
Breast harness 161
Breeding
  ancient Greeks, by 68
  conditions 92-3

different species 30
domestic animals 30
injury, risk of 87
natural conditions, under 86-7
responsibility, taking 89
selective 6 9-70
Breeds
    number of 68
    types of 78
Bridles 148-9
Bridling 147
Bruises 181
Byerley, Captain 75-6
Byerley Turk 75-6

Camarero 150
Camargue horses 57, 71
Carriages 160-1, 163
Cavalettis 135-6,137
Cave paintings 26, 28, 29
Cavesson 135, 148
Centaur 44
Chambon 127
Chariot horses, training 159-60
Chariots 32-3
Childwick Bury 109
Chinese cavalry men 37
Chiron 44
Circulatory system 17
Clydesdale 78, 80
Colour perception 64-6
Communication 54-6 4
Contusions 181

Cortijo de Quarto stud farm 108
Cross-country 153
Crusades 38
Curb bit 149

Dappled horses 69
Darley Arabian 75-6
Darley, Thomas 76
Dartmoor ponies 69, 84
Dawn horses 22
Deserts, horses in 69
Digestion 96, 98
Digestive tract, problems with 182
Dnjepr River 28
Domestic horse, origin of 29-33
Domestication of the horse 28-9
Donkeys 41
Draught animal 32, 78, 159
Draw reins 125-6
Dressage 128, 137-40
Drinking 101
Driving 159-60, 164
Droppings
    identification by 61
    pile, as demonstration of rank 61
Dülmen wild horses 109

Eclipse 76
Eczema 178-9
Endurance 20
English riding style 128-9
English saddle 140, 142
Eocene period 22

Eohippus 22
Equus asinus 30
Equus przewalskii 29
Equus przewalskii gmelini 30
Equus przewalskii grazilis 30
Equus przewalskii silvaticus 30
Etruscans 34
Eurasia, horses in 23
European riding style 128-9, 132
European saddle 140
Exercise machines 107
Exmoor ponies 32, 69, 71
Exterior, the 6
Eyes 64, 65
    conjunctiva 177
    dull or inflamed 177

Falabella ponies, Argentinean 85
Feeding 21
    assimilation of nourishment 98
    barley 98, 100
    bulk food 99
    changing environment, adapting to 94
    concentrated foodstuff 99
    digestion 96, 98
    fussiness 95
    grain 94-5
    grass, diet of 94, 99
    grazing 95, 96
    hay 100
    leaves and bark 95
    maize 98, 100
    mangers, positioning 104

202

mouth, using 95-6
number and quality of meals 99
oats 98, 101
roughage 99-100
rye 98, 100
salt licks 101
small horses 100-1
wheat 98, 100
Fiaschi, Cesare 38
First-aid kit 180
Fjord ponies 78, 84, 117
Flies 178, 179
Flight, horse built for 20
Foals
    birth of 86, 88
    communication 58
    exercise 88, 92
    hierarchy, in 49
    independence 91
    mother, bond with 90-1
    other horses, playing with 92
    pasture land for 92
    raising 88-93
Forest tarpan 30, 69
Founder 185
Freiberger 78, 81

Gaits 118
Gallop 118, 119
Gazelle Horn 42-3
Gelding 91
Godolphin Barb 75-8
Greeks, role of horses for 33
Grevy zebra 47-8
Grisone, Frederico 38, 128
Grooming 54
    body brush 111

body contact 112, 114
cleaning box 110
coat, mane and tail 114-17
curry comb 111
feet, cleaning 113
hoof pick 110
hooves, oiling 112
legs 110
need for 110
showers 112
Gymkhana 173

Hackamore, American 148
Haflinger 70, 78
Hanover Shoe Farms 109
Harness races 143, 152
Hay 100
Health 176-87
Hearing 63
Heart 21
Helmets 189, 195
Herds 46-52
Hinny 30
Hooves
    development of 23
    looking after 185
    oiling 112
Horse behaviour
    communication 54-61
    danger, reaction to 65, 66
    disturbed 107
    ears, positions of 57-8, 60, 63
    faeces pile, significance of 61
    friendships 49, 53, 55
    groups, living in 46-52
    greeting each other 60
    humans, friendship with 53-4, 67

language 58
mood barometer 57
nibbling 114
pecking order 48-9, 52-3
rank, demonstrations of 61
relationships 48-9, 52-3, 55
threatening gestures 60
tolerance 53-4
wild, in 52
Horse's hair 114-17
Horse-drawn wagon 163
Horse-driving 164, 166
Horseflies 178
Horsepower 165
Horseracing 143, 150
Horsetail 102
Humans and horses, relationship of 23-8
Huns 37
Hyksos dynasty 32
Hyracotherium 22-23

Ice Age 23, 26
Icelandic ponies 69, 78, 84, 118-20
Identifying horses 195
Indoor riding track, riding on 188
Internal organs 16
Iron mask, protective 34

Jacobson's organ 58
Jockeys 156
Karnak, temple at 31
Kikkuli 159-60
Kincsem 150
Knights 38

Laburnum 103
Laminitis 185

Large horses, need for 31
Lascaux 28, 29
Le Pin 108
Leg injuries 21
Legs 20-1
Liability insurance 194-5
Long-distance riding and racing 166-8
Lunging 133-5
Lungs 21
Lupin 103

Macedonian mountain horse 85
Mangers, positioning 104
Marbach, stud farm 108
Mares 91
Mating
    capitivity, in 87-8
    exhibitionism 90
    fertility, altering time of 88
    mating period 88, 92
Meadow saffron 102-3
Mohammed 71
Monotony 190-1
Mounted games 168, 169-73
Mules 30
    breeding 36
Musculature 16
Mustang 79

National stud farm 109
Neck 21
Neighing 60

Oak 103

Pacing gait 118
Palio 43

204
Parthenon 32
Paso horses 118, 121
Pegasus 33
Percheron 78, 80
Persians, dappled horses 69
Peruvian cavesson 148
Piggot, Lester 156
Pinto 80
Plaiting 114
Pluvinel, Antoine de 40, 128-9
Poisonous plants 102-3
Polo 171
Ponies
    feeding 100-1
    meaning 78
Portuguese saddle 145
Predators 66
Prehistoric horses 21, 22, 26
Przewalski's horse 26, 29, 70
Pulse, checking 176, 177

Quadrilles 156-9
Quarter horse 81-2, 86, 87

Reproductive period 48
Respiration 176
Respiratory ailments 182
Riding outdoors 188-90
Riding reins 125-7
Riding styles 128-33
Ringworm 178-9, 181
Robinia 103
Rolling 53
Roman Empire 34, 36-7
Running martingale 127
Running muscles 20

Saddle pad 146
Saddles 140, 142-3
    poorly-fitting 181
Saddling 146
St John's wort 102
Salt licks 101
Scyphios 33
Shetland pony 32, 69, 84
Shire horses, English 85
Shoemaker, Willie 156
Side reins 125
Siena 43
Sight 63, 64-6
Skeleton 17
Smells
    absorbing 58
    sense of smell 61, 64
Snaffle bridle 149
Solutre 23
South American bridle 148
Spanish riding style 129
Spectacular Bid 150
Speed 20
Sporting gaits 122
Sporting horses 79
Stabling
    boxes 104, 106, 107
    group enclosure 106
    open stables 106-7
    traditional 104
    windows and doors, leaving open 108
Stagecoach 163
Stallions 91
    communication 58
    family, influence on 48
    fighting 86, 88-9
    fights 61

mating 87
sounds 60
Standing martingale 125
Star Appeal 150
Steeplechasing 153
Steppe tarpan 29-30, 69
Steppes 69
Stomach 96
Stud farms 108-9
Sweating 176
Swedish sporting horse 82

Teeth 21
Tellington touch 186
Tenessee Walking Horse 117
Association 122
Therapy
horses, for 186-7
riding as 124
Thoroughbreds
Arab 70-1, 72-73
English 70-8
Three-day event 150-6
Ticks 178
Tolt 118, 119
Touring saddle 144
Traffic rules 194
Trail riding 174
Trakener 83
Transporting horses 191, 194
Travelling by horse 32
Trot 118
Trotting 143
Tundra horses 80
Turkish officer's saddle 144
Twitch, the 86

Unicorn 42-3

Vaqueros 129
Vaulting 123
Vienna's Spanish Riding School 40

Walk 118
Water dropwort 103
Water hemlock 103
Weights, record 85
Welsh ponies 85
Western horses 79-86
Western riding 129-32, 133, 174, 175
halter 175
reining 174
showmanship 174
sport of 173-5
superhorse 174
Western pleasure 174
Western saddle 142-3
girth 146
Wild asses 41
Wild, horses returning to 31-2
Winter coats 107-8
Women, riding by 45
Worms 178
Wounds 181
Würtemmberg 83

Xenophon 36

Yawning 64
Yew 103

Zebras 22

ACKNOWLEDGEMENTS

The publishers wish to acknowledge the following people for their
contributions to the book

————

Bettina Koelliker

Hans-Beat Koelliker

Kim Dossenbach

Nina Dossenbach

Robert Buchmüller

Sabine Meier

Urs Aregger

————

PICTURE CREDITS

PHOTOGRAPHS

Foto -Agentur-Sutter Jacana & Explorer, Paris/Michel: 29 *tl*; R Sidney: 29 *tr*;
Ph Masse: 21 *r*

Archiv für Kunst und Geschichtre, Berlin: 38-39

British Museum, London: 30-31, 32, 33, 35, 37

Severino Dahint/Natural History Museum Basel: 24-25

Claudia Feh: 26, 46-47, 49, 52, 55 *tr*, 56-57, 60, 68, 71, 95

Istituto Scala, Florence: 36

Foto Löbl-Schleyer: 34

The Mansell Collection: 44

Beatrice Michel: 41, 54-55, 61, 64, 89, 94

Animal Hospital Bern, Clinic for Domestic Animals and Horses: 177 *t*, *cl*, *c*, 179, 180, 185

Zefa/Dr F Sauer: 28

All other photographs are the property of Monika and Hans D Dossenbach

---

ILLUSTRATIONS

John Michael Davis/Michael Beazley Int'l Publishers: 102 (2,3) 103 (4,5,7)

Hunt & Sons (1860): 45

Beatrice Michel: 100, 101, 125, 126, 136

Crispin de Passe (1622): 40

Derek St Romaine/Michell Beazley Int'l Publishers: 102 (1), 103 (6,8,)

Ludovico Vartoman (1515): 42

Elizabeth Zellweger-Schroer: 6,7,9,11,13, 16, 17, 21

———